Creating Space for Conflicted Histories: Remembering the Atomic Bomb

By

Raffi E. Andonian

First Printing: 2020

ISBN: 978-0-9963197-7-5

Cronus Media Ventures, LLC
Columbus, Ohio

Epoch Publishing
San Diego, CA

www.CronusMediaVentures.com

www.RaffiAndonian.com

Cover Photo Credit: T. Harmon Parkhurst, Courtesy of the Los Alamos Historical Society Photo Archives

Dedication

To Scott Hartwig of Gettysburg as my mentor in historical interpretation,

To Heather McClenahan of Los Alamos for her leadership in telling these stories,

And thanks to both for their support in anything I endeavor.

Table of Contents

Foreword

The cliché states that political divisions in the United States have never been worse than they are today. Historically speaking, that is simply not true. Post-Revolutionary America, the Civil War, and the Civil Rights Movement were truly life and death schisms within our country. Still, divisiveness seems to rule the day, precisely because of its accessibility—whether viral videos of mobs tearing down statues, anonymous vitriol spewed on internet comment boards, or social media memes that attempt to distil complicated ideas into the thoughts of a cat.

One in five Americans say a friendship has been damaged as the result of a political argument, and psychology magazines spend pages, especially around elections, urging readers not to drop friends who disagree with them. Antebellum plantations are criticized for showing the difficulties of slaves' lives rather than the glamor of Southern living, and a founding member of Greenpeace who comes out in support of non-carbon-polluting nuclear power gets raked over the proverbial coals by former colleagues. Where then, can one turn to have a civil discussion about a disagreeable topic?

Historic sites can and should be at the forefront of these discussions. They offer a sense of place and a setting where multiple ideas and interpretations can be shared. These sites have a responsibility, in fact, to ensure visitors have opportunities to access information as well as share their own ideas and experiences.

Having worked at both Gettysburg and Los Alamos, Raffi Andonian has been on the front lines of battles related to complicated histories. Because of the multiple perspectives and interactive opportunities offered at these particular sites, he also has had opportunities to see visitors, young and old, come away with new perspectives and new understandings of history. Even if their fundamental views do not change, at least for a time they have opened their thoughts to ideas to which they might never otherwise have been exposed.

Creating Space for Conflicted Histories: Remembering the Atomic Bomb comes at a decisive time in the nation's political discourse. A case study on the contentious creation of the Manhattan Project National Historical Park, it urges us to ask questions and reflect rather than spout answers and argue. It also offers a path forward for historic sites to lead these discussions through thought-provoking questions that do not have easy answers.

As educators and interpreters, Raffi and I both hope to see this book used to begin deep discussions and dialogs. We anticipate sites and their visitors will explore the questions Raffi poses and come to greater, more nuanced understandings of difficult and complex histories. We believe historic sites can lead the way toward bringing people together rather than exacerbating differences. And maybe—just maybe—such deliberations can help heal some of the divisions that are so evident today.

Heather McClenahan
Retired Executive Director
Los Alamos Historical Society

Introduction: Space for Dialogue

How we remember historic events shapes how we view our society, political framework, and our place in the world. Consider recent issues regarding Confederate monuments, reparations for American slavery, the role of identity in politics, and subsequent polarization of national dialogue. These complicated matters are often simplified by opposing sides into neat, meme-worthy positions, with uncomplicated messages playing on who we think we ought to be, based on a perception of who we think we have been, from whence we came, and how that shapes our current society. This power of historical memory manifests in regularly occurring fights over school textbooks and curricula, public portrayals of historical figures, and the framework of remembrance for historic events.

The creation and use of the atomic bomb—born of the Manhattan Project during the Second World War—and its resulting nuclear history, has long been a controversial topic. The use of the bomb was debated even before its creation, and for decades since, disputes surrounding nuclear technology have continued in various contexts: warfare, diplomacy, energy, healthcare, and environment. This contested memory is one reason the decade-long effort to create the Manhattan Project National Historical Park failed in September 2012. Although the park ultimately was established later as part of the 2015 National Defense

Authorization Act (NDAA), the debate about it revealed opposing narratives based on layers of nuclear legacies, stemming from 1945 through the present, pervading the public's historical memory of the Manhattan Project.

The years of efforts to organize the park, its failure in Congress as a bill (and later passage as part of a defense spending bill), and the discussions about it raised many questions: What is worth preserving? What is the meaning of our national parks? How do we interpret narratives of contested memory? What do these narratives say about who we are and who we wish to become as a society?

Creating space for dialogue about places with complicated histories is perhaps the leading reason to advocate for their protection and interpretation. Remembrance of the stories surrounding the atomic bomb and the subsequent narratives of nuclear history provide a case study on the challenges of telling these stories. A closer look at this globally significant history, along with the way we choose to remember it, provides some insight into how we may choose to deal with sites that have pasts now seen as controversial. In this era of political polarization and of rhetoric dismissive of the "other" side, do places with complex stories provide a unique capability for creating much needed conversations?

Indeed, these scarce forums for discussion should become even more cherished. Establishing places to interpret many narratives creates spaces in which willing participants may have conversations with family or strangers that they might otherwise never have—triggered by place, environment, education, interpretation, and reflection. The relevance of creating dialogue on conflicted histories with the power of place, now when so little space for understanding each other exists, becomes important today more than ever.

Interpreting the history of the atomic bomb provides a case study about how we might evaluate historical memories in public spaces. Its implications could affect how we view Confederate monuments, sites of the Jim Crow era and civil rights struggles, the likeness of historic figures with pasts of which we now disapprove, and other sites that represent apartheid, fascism, totalitarianism, and more. Therefore, the chapters that follow have been organized by the guiding questions we may apply to each of these circumstances:

- Why remember?
- What is the history to be remembered?
- What does it mean to remember?
- How to remember?

These questions—in this sequence—allow us to consider the significance, the accuracy, the meaning, and the messaging for each particular circumstance. It can then provide a guide for contested historic sites beyond the one examined here, which will, in turn, demonstrate the validity of the process.

Chapter 1: Why Remember?

"The ability to split atoms and extract energy from them was one of the more remarkable scientific achievements of the 20th century, widely seen as world-changing," reported *The Economist*, a leading global publication. "Intuitively," the newspaper continued, "one might expect such a scientific wonder either to sweep all before it or be renounced, rather than end up in a modest niche, at best stable, at worst dwindling." However, historic and social contexts have shaped the fate of the technology: "If nuclear power teaches one lesson, it is to doubt all stories of technological determinism. It is not the essential nature of a technology that matters but its capacity to fit into the social, political and economic conditions of the day." With its extensive Special Report assessment of nuclear energy in 2012, *The Economist* revealed just how relevant, charged, and yet ambivalent nuclear history remains. "To the public at large," the report gauged, "the history of nuclear power is mostly a history of accidents." Even in the twenty-first century, the 2011 disaster at Fukushima in Japan seemed to demonstrate that cold reality. Thus, nuclear power continues as "a creature of politics not economics."[1]

---

[1] "The Dream that Failed," Special Report on Nuclear Energy, *The Economist*, 10 March 2012.

Nearly seven decades after the only wartime use of nuclear weapons, the political implications of all things nuclear make it a difficult topic to discuss in public forums. Thus, when United States President Barack Obama called for "an all-out, all-of-the-above strategy that develops every available source of American energy," he avoided mentioning nuclear energy, despite the fact that one-fifth of the electricity in the United States is supplied by its 104 nuclear reactors. In spite of U.S. dependence on nuclear energy, almost two-thirds of Americans oppose building new nuclear reactors, and it remains a politically unpopular issue. Globally, nuclear power provided 13 percent of the world's electricity in 2010—although that number was down from 18 percent in 1996. Even in Japan, site of the world's first victims of nuclear weapons, 30 percent of electricity in 2010 derived from nuclear power, a source in use there since the 1960s. For example, art referencing nuclear bombs in Japan remains taboo, even insulting and offensive.

The world's three most memorable nuclear accidents—Three Mile Island in 1979, Chernobyl in 1986, and Fukushima in 2011—stir up questions about the validity of nuclear energy. In the realm of foreign policy, the political power of nuclear arms remains apparent well after the end of the Cold War, as "worries about the dark side of nuclear power are resurgent, thanks to what is happening in Iran."[2] The

---

[2] *The Economist* had recently published a series of articles

13

domestic front is even more controversial, as confirmed by President Obama's comments and omission, particularly considering the mood created by fresh memories from Fukushima and by opposition to new projects in the United States allowed by the Nuclear Regulatory Commission. As *The Economist* surmised, "America's anti-nuclear movement has been as quiet as its nuclear industry, but as one comes to life so will the other."[3]

Within this climate, morally perplexing since the development of the first nuclear weapons in 1945, came yet another issue that triggered strong public reaction about the nuclear legacy. Following several years of planning and study, and several months of effort in Congress to introduce and pass it, the Manhattan Project National Historical Park Act failed in the U.S. House of Representatives in September 2012. The legislation would have created a non-contiguous unit to be added to the National Park Service (NPS). The park would not acquire any property, but a visitor center would have been established in each of three locations to interpret

---

about Iran's nuclear capabilities (and surrounding politics and diplomacy), which was popular during the 2012 election cycle. See the 25 February 2012 issue just weeks prior to the Special Report on Nuclear Energy.

[3] "Nuclear Power: The 30-Year Itch," *The Economist*, 18 February 2012; "The Dream that Failed," Special Report on Nuclear Energy, *The Economist*, 10 March 2012; "Art after Fukushima," *The Economist*, 10 March 2012.

existing U.S. Department of Energy sites: Oak Ridge, Tennessee; Hanford, Washington; and Los Alamos, New Mexico. These locations were critical to the Manhattan Project, which created the world's first nuclear weapons in an effort to bring a swift end to the Second World War. The visitor centers would include information and interpretation (both formal and informal), offer exhibits and tours, and direct visitors to partners already present in the community, such as the Los Alamos History Museum or the Bradbury Science Museum in Los Alamos, site of the Manhattan Project's chief laboratory facility. A struggle over how to understand nuclear history—where it fit in United States and world history, and how it should be remembered—had been triggered by the park legislation.

The historiography of the nuclear bombs produced by the Manhattan Project is a divided one with many underlying emotions, politics, and contestations. Within a decade of the use of the atomic bomb and the end of the Second World War, Gar Alperovitz challenged the narrative that its use was to end the war and instead argued that its purpose was to intimidate the Soviet Union. His contemporary, Herbert Feis, had already argued in support of the official story: the aim of the use of the bomb was to end the war with the fastest pace and fewest American casualties possible. A generation later, historians led by Richard Rhodes, Robert James Maddox, and Robert Newman maintained this basic contention in response to revisionist interpretations like that of Alperovitz. They argued that the

Manchurian invasion by the Soviet Union was not enough to prevent the need for the U.S. invasion of Japan. Thus, the bomb succeeded in averting a bloody invasion. David McCullough and Alonzo Hamby, biographers of President Harry S. Truman, who held the ultimate power to make the decision to drop the bombs, agreed with this interpretation. Alperovitz responded—along with others, such as Dennis Wainstock and a host of essayists in a volume edited by Kai Bird and Lawrence Lifschultz—by claiming that the United States had portrayed the use of the atomic bomb as an acceptable alternative by overlooking that Japan was ready to surrender, delaying involvement by the Soviet Union and then diminishing its significance, and aggrandizing the number of American casualties expected in a potential invasion of Japan. John Dower and Ronald Takaki applied race as their primary analytical lens, citing Truman's racial views regarding Japanese and the larger cultural context of American dehumanization of Japanese people, which made the use of the atomic bomb less uncomfortable than it might have been against an enemy like Germany. Thus, historical interpretation remains divided.[4]

---

[4] Gar Alperovitz, *Atomic Diplomacy: Hiroshima and Potsdam: The Use of the Atomic Bomb and the American Confrontation with Soviet Power* (New York: Simon & Schuster, 1965); Herbert Feis, *The Atomic Bomb and the End of World War II* (Princeton: Princeton University Press, 1961, 1966); Richard Rhodes, *The Making of the Atomic Bomb* (New York: Simon & Schuster, 1986);

These debates about the past are rooted in the present. As the anthropologist Richard Flores explains, "Stories of the past envelop us: they inscribe our present and shape our future; stories of the past are linked to the formation of selves and others in a complex tapestry of textured narratives." Viewed from the present, the past pervades the current and contemporary—the now. "Remembering is a deeply embedded social practice that informs the present," according to Flores. J. E. Tunbridge and G. J.

Robert James Maddox, *Weapons for Victory: The Hiroshima Decision Fifty Years Later* (Columbia: University of Missouri Press, 1995); Robert P. Newman, *Truman and the Hiroshima Cult* (East Lansing: Michigan State University Press, 1995); David McCullough, *Truman* (New York: Simon & Schuster, 1992); Alonzo L. Hamby, *Man of the People: A Life of Harry S. Truman* (New York: Oxford University Press, 1995); Gar Alperovitz, *The Decision to Use the Atomic Bomb and the Architecture of an American Myth* (New York: Alfred A. Knopf, 1995); Dennis D. Wainstock, *The Decision to Drop the Atomic Bomb* (Westport: Praeger Publishers, 1996); Kai Bird and Lawrence Lifschultz, eds., *Hiroshima's Shadow* (Stony Creek: Pamphleteer's Press, 1998); John Dower, *War Without Mercy: Race and Power in the Pacific War* (New York: Pantheon, 1986); Ronald Takaki, *Hiroshima: Why America Dropped the Atomic Bomb* (Boston: Little, Brown & Company, 1995). For an overview of historiography about the decision to drop the world's first nuclear weapon, see: J. Samuel Walker, "Recent Literature on Truman's Atomic Bomb Decision: A Search for Middle Ground," *Diplomatic History*, Vol. 29, No. 2, April 2005, pp. 311-334.

Ashworth, international scholars of heritage tourism, delineate further distinctions while maintaining an understanding of remembrance similar to that of Flores: "History is what a historian regards as worth recording and heritage is what contemporary society chooses to inherit and to pass on." That is, "the past" is "what has happened," "history" is "selective attempts to describe this [past]," and "heritage" is "a contemporary product shaped from history." The heritage of atrocity, according to Tunbridge and Ashworth, carries particular importance and intensity:

> *It is disproportionately significant to many heritage users. Its memory can so dominate the heritage of individuals or social and political groups, as to have profound effects upon their self-conscious identity to the extent that it may become almost a sine qua non of group cohesion in sects, tribes or states, powerfully motivating their self-image and aspirations, over many centuries... The dissonance created by the interpretation of atrocity is not only particularly intense and lasting but also particularly complex for victims, perpetrators and observers.*[5]

---

[5] Richard Flores, *Remembering the Alamo: Memory, Modernity, and the Master Symbol* (Austin: University of Texas Press, 2002), x, xvi; J. E. Tunbridge and G. J. Ashworth, *Dissonant Heritage: The Management of the Past as a Resource in Conflict* (Chichester: John Wiley & Sons, 1996), 6, 20, 94, 95.

Interpreting the immediate outcomes of the Manhattan Project—victory versus defeat, lives saved versus lives lost, perceptions of good versus evil, the end of a world war versus the beginning of a new kind of war—reveals just how complex, multifaceted, sensitive, dissonant, and influential historical memory, understanding, and interpretation can become. The eminent geographer David Lowenthal points out, "Heritage is mandatory. It comes to us willy-nilly, and cannot be shed however shaming it may be." Despite a failure by prior generations of historic preservationists to consider a variety of perspectives, as indicated by the interdisciplinary academicians Max Page and Randall Mason, "they can now be part of the ongoing reevaluation of American history." Art historians Robert Nelson and Margaret Olin note, "All complex societies, it may be argued, invest cultural and actual capital in structures akin to monuments." The Manhattan Project National Historical Park is simultaneously what Alois Riegl, the first Conservator General of monuments in the Austro-Hungarian Empire, described over a century ago as an "intentional monument" (the park itself with significance determined by the creators) and an "unintentional monument" (the project that became a monument only as a product of later events rather than the full intent of the historical actors)—in essence, an intentional monument to an unintentional monument.[6]

---

[6] David Lowenthal, "The Heritage Crusade and Its

Historical understanding, particularly about such textured stories, relies on a sense of place—the power of place. Heritage anthropologist Barbara Bender explains, "People's sense of place and landscape thus extends out from the locale and from the present encounter and is contingent upon a larger temporal and spatial field of relationships." More than half a century ago, Freeman Tilden, whose work captured the philosophy and substance of interpretation still used as a foundation today, highlighted the deep connection of understanding intangible concepts at a tangible location: "A kind of elective education that is superior in some respects to that of the classroom, for here he meets the Thing Itself." More recently, in analyzing a different contested history with much impact, power, memory, and mythology, anthropologist Flores remarks about

---

Contradictions," in Max Page and Randall Mason, eds., *Giving Preservation a History: Histories of Historic Preservation in the United States* (New York: Routledge, 2004), 20; Max Page and Randall Mason, "Rethinking the Roots of the Historic Preservation Movement," in Max Page and Randall Mason, eds., *Giving Preservation a History: Histories of Historic Preservation in the United States* (New York: Routledge, 2004), 15; Robert S. Nelson and Margaret Olin, "Introduction," in Robert S. Nelson and Margaret Olin, eds., *Monuments and Memory, Made and Unmade* (Chicago: University of Chicago Press, 2003), 4; Alois Riegl, "The Modern Cult of Monuments: Its Character and Its Origin," translated by Forster and Ghirardo, *Oppositions* 25 (Fall 1982), pp. 21-56.

his experience, applicable to the geopolitically and culturally influential history and memory of the Manhattan Project: "Because of the interreferentiality between the cultural memory of the Alamo and the place itself, the full force of this site can only be experienced ethnographically, which is to say, by one's presence." Art historians Nelson and Olin recognize the power of monuments (which a national park might be considered), "Social processes surrounding the monument begin even before it is seen. Travel to the monument, like all forms of pilgrimage, transforms object and beholder." Thus, William Murtagh, the first Keeper of the National Register of Historic Places, observed that efforts in historic preservation continue to increase "thanks to an ever-enlarging preservation-oriented constituency which comprehends the value of retaining the sense of time, place, and locality in a country of great diversity and vast dimensions." Whereas nineteenth-century historic preservation was fueled by "patriotism... to the exclusion of any of the other interests," today "the federal government's role in preservation grew" to what it has become with many diversified concerns in mind.[7]

---

[7] Barbara Bender, "Introduction," in Barbara Bender and Margot Winer, eds., *Contested Landscapes: Movement, Exile and Place* (Oxford: Berg, 2001), 6; Greg Dickinson, Carole Blair, and Brian L. Ott, "Rhetoric/Memory/Place," in Greg Dickinson, Carole Blair, and Brian L. Ott, eds., *Places of Public Memory: The Rhetoric of Museums and Memorials* (Tuscaloosa: University of Alabama Press,

The roles of publicly protected hallowed spaces and the significance of sense of place in influencing historical understanding have changed over time. Edward Linenthal, a professor of religious studies who explores the creation of the meanings of public symbols, delineates two ways contested historic sites like battlefields continue to function in the United States:

> *On the one hand, they are ceremonial centers where various forms of veneration reflect the belief that the contemporary power and relevance of the 'lessons' of the battle are crucial for the continued life of the nation. Furthermore, many people believe that the patriotic inspiration to be extracted from these sacred places depends not only on proper ceremony but on memorialized, preserved, restored, and purified environment. On the other hand, these battle sites are civil spaces*

2010), 32; Freeman Tilden, *Interpreting Our Heritage* (Chapel Hill: University of North Carolina Press, 1957, 1967, 1977, 2007), 25; Richard Flores, *Remembering the Alamo: Memory, Modernity, and the Master Symbol* (Austin: University of Texas Press, 2002), 20; Robert S. Nelson and Margaret Olin, "Introduction," in Robert S. Nelson and Margaret Olin, eds., *Monuments and Memory, Made and Unmade* (Chicago: University of Chicago Press, 2003), 6; William J. Murtagh, *Keeping Time: The History and Theory of Preservation in America* (New York: Sterling Publishing Co., 1988), 165, 12.

where Americans of various ideological persuasions come, not always reverently, to compete for the ownership of powerful national stories and to argue about the nature of heroism, the meaning of war, the efficacy of martial sacrifice, and the significance of preserving the patriotic landscape to the nation.

Clearly, the meaning of a historic site with contested history is not universally agreed upon by the American public, which leaves much room for debate. This debate justifies the very presence and function of the site, as interpretation can help visitors contemplate the meanings of such places. In his landmark work on historic preservation, James Marston Fitch called attention to the fact that "before modern times, the enjoyment and consumption of most cultural artifacts were public acts." Despite a period of the privatization of the cultural artifact, Fitch emphasized, "It is safe to assume that every independent nation in the world today is committed, at least in principle, to the theory that the protection of the national artistic and historic heritage is a responsibility of the state." Fitch asserted, "Organized society has always recognized the educational role of historic sites and monuments."[8]

---

[8] Edward Tabor Linenthal, *Sacred Ground: Americans and Their Battlefields* (Champaign: University of Illinois Press, 1991, 1993), 1; James Marston Fitch, *Historic Preservation: Curatorial Management of the Built World*

In the United States, the National Park Service has been the chief federal organ of historic preservation, since the New Deal era. By the 1920s, the NPS began, as environmental historian Alfred Runte puts it, "to look beyond its traditional role... by actively promoting additions to the system whose significance was distinctly historical or archaeological rather than scenic." During his term as the second director of the National Park Service, Horace M. Albright "campaigned for recognition of the agency as the appropriate custodian of all federal historic and archaeological sites." After a meeting between Albright and Franklin Delano Roosevelt in 1933, the president signed an executive order that transferred sixty-four national monuments, military parks, battlefield sites, cemeteries, and memorials from the Department of War, U.S. Forest Service, and District of Columbia to the NPS, instantly doubling the size of the national park system. As historian Denise Meringolo maintains, Albright's "understanding of the park service mission, his vision for expansion, and his political savvy enabled the transformation of a landscape long defined as scenic and scientific into one that might be recognized as historic." With the increase of domestic tourism to national parks over the following decades, NPS professionals "were idealistic, believing park education could open visitors to new experiences." These sites were no longer merely monuments of

(New York: McGraw-Hill, 1982), 3, 399, 403.

reverence but became places of education through the implementation of new approaches that avoided simple confirmation of what visitors already believed prior to their arrival.[9]

Consequently, the NPS underwent a transformation between the 1930s era of the New Deal and the 1960s era of the National Historic Preservation Act. With the issuance of Executive Order 6166 by President Roosevelt, "the responsibility for preservation within the federal government" became "transferred" to the National Park Service, as historian Hal Rothman analyzes the historical moment. Rothman understands the 1933 reorganization of the National Park Service made the body "a national entity with responsibility for much more than scenery." These groundbreaking developments "put the agency in the field of historic preservation in a manner that no federal agency had previously attempted," argues Rothman, placing the National Park Service at the "forefront of historic preservation." The political thrust redefined not only the roles of the National Park Service and the larger federal government in historic preservation but also Americans' cultural conceptions of the United States.

---

[9] Alfred Runte, *National Parks: The American Experience* (Lincoln: University of Nebraska Press, 1979, 1987), 219, 219-220; Denise D. Meringolo, *Museums, Monuments, and National Parks: Toward a New Genealogy of Public History* (Amherst: University of Massachusetts Press, 2012), xxxi.

This revolution meant, according to Rothman, "Americans no longer had to look to Europe and the ancient world to see their cultural roots. The North American continent had a human past worthy of consideration." In essence, the organized federal effort in historic preservation created a history and a memory—a heritage.[10]

In the case of the use of the world's first nuclear weapons, remembering the history and forming a heritage has already proven a contentious challenge. To commemorate the fiftieth anniversary of the dropping of the first atomic bomb on Hiroshima, the National Air and Space Museum (NASM), a Smithsonian Institution, prepared an exhibit to debut in 1995 about the impacts of this weapon, with the *Enola Gay*, the plane that carried the atomic bomb to Hiroshima in 1945, as its centerpiece. The exhibit never came to fruition. Richard Kohn, a prominent military historian who worked as the chief of air force history for the U.S. Air Force and served on multiple advisory committees for the NASM, later captured the conflicting symbolism of the *Enola Gay* "emphasizing either innovative technological achievement or the mass death of enemy civilians." Edward Linenthal, who served on the advisory committee of the NASM for the exhibit, identified the

---

[10] Hal Rothman, *America's National Monuments: The Politics of Preservation* (Lawrence: University Press of Kansas, 1989), 187, 209, 208-209.

crux of these differing stories "of a weapon that brought peace and victory, and of a weapon that brought destruction and fear to the world." These emotionally charged and sometimes ideologically driven disagreements about constructing heritage led to a national debate in 1995 filled with such vitriol that it "reminds us the ways in which the cultural fallout from the bomb that destroyed Hiroshima still reaches into our own time, of how we continue to underestimate the destabilizing force of the blast." Despite Linenthal's experience working on projects with volatile histories and fiery memories such as Pearl Harbor and the United States Holocaust Memorial Museum, the reaction to the planned exhibit about the *Enola Gay* and the atomic bomb was so explosive that Linenthal later admitted that "Nothing in my experience with memorial exhibits prepared me for what happened."[11] Opposition to the

---

[11] Richard H. Kohn, "History at Risk: The Case of the *Enola Gay*," in Edward T. Linenthal and Tom Engelhardt, eds., *History Wars: The Enola Gay and Other Battles for the American Past* (New York: Henry Holt and Company, 1996), 145; Tom Engelhardt and Edward T. Linenthal, "Introduction: History Under Siege," in Edward T. Linenthal and Tom Engelhardt, eds., *History Wars: The Enola Gay and Other Battles for the American Past* (New York: Henry Holt and Company, 1996), 2, 6; Edward T. Linenthal, "Anatomy of a Controversy," in Edward T. Linenthal and Tom Engelhardt, eds., *History Wars: The Enola Gay and Other Battles for the American Past* (New York: Henry Holt and Company, 1996), 10. For a scholarly monograph about the *Enola Gay* exhibit and its

exhibit stemmed mostly from veterans groups, who believed the focus on the bomb's destruction rather than the Japanese wartime aggression and atrocities, did not represent "true" history.

Nearly two decades later, opposition to public remembrance of the origins, impact, and legacies surrounding the world's first nuclear weapons would again block federal efforts to recognize this history. In 2012, the Manhattan Project National Historical Park Act failed to get enough votes in the U.S. House of Representatives. The bill would have created the Manhattan Project National Historical Park, dedicated to protecting the key sites of arguably the most significant event of the twentieth-century that reshaped the history of the world in multiple ways. This time, however, the concerns raised in protest were from the opposite side, those fearing glorification of nuclear weapons rather than too much veneration of American enemies. In the case of the *Enola Gay* exhibit in 1995, "veterans' groups, political commentators, social critics, and politicians had charged that the exhibition script dishonored the Americans who fought the war by questioning the motives for using the bombs, by portraying the bombs as unnecessary to end the war, and by sympathizing too much with the Japanese killed by the bombs and, by implication, with the Japanese cause." In 2012,

cultural implications about historical memory, see: Robert P. Newman, *Enola Gay and the Court of History* (New York: Peter Lang Publishing, 2004).

publicly-voiced opposition to the Manhattan Project National Historical Park came from those who worried that protecting these sites, particularly by designation as national treasures through the National Park Service, would mean celebrating the use of the bomb in the past and possibly in the future via simplistic narratives about American achievement, triumph, and righteousness. The subsequent public debate raised questions about the role of historic preservation, the meaning of national parks, and the legacies of the atomic bomb.[12]

Nuclear history remains contentious because it has cost many lives and public attention focuses on famous accidents. In particular, the Manhattan Project National Historical Park sparked sharp reactions because of the underlying question of whether the dropping of the bombs made strategic and moral sense. The Manhattan Project itself was so focused on developing the science and engineering necessary to end the war that many of its participants likely did not foresee its impact for decades to come. Still, the historical memory of this event remains driven by perceptions of the Second World War and the hindsight of the effects of the Cold War and beyond. The impact of the Manhattan Project on these

---

[12] Richard H. Kohn, "History at Risk: The Case of the *Enola Gay*," in Edward T. Linenthal and Tom Engelhardt, eds., *History Wars: The Enola Gay and Other Battles for the American Past* (New York: Henry Holt and Company, 1996), 140.

historically defining eras makes a compelling case for validity of the Manhattan Project National Historical Park. The National Park Service has proven that it is equipped to take on the difficult task of both preserving resources and interpreting stories with many perspectives. It has shown that it can fairly interpret the many narratives that become evident from the process of the public debate.

Debating the meanings of the Manhattan Project National Historical Park reveals that the field of historic preservation must continue to uphold a high standard and perhaps even elevate its advocacy when it comes to nuclear histories. Failing to do so undermines the credibility of historic preservation as having advanced beyond mere glorification. Omitting the Manhattan Project National Historical Park due to opposition to nuclear politics would serve to reinforce the notion of preserving only that history which a nation decides as worth exalting, because it would avoid confronting the reality of the past of the United States so influenced by nuclear history.

Much of the debate surrounding the legitimacy of creating the Manhattan Project National Historical Park became focused on an ethical question about whether or not using nuclear weapons on Japan was morally justified and strategically necessary to end World War II. This underlying question will never have a definitive answer, and thus, historians and the public will never reach a consensus. This is all the more reason for the creation of more sites like this one—the ongoing dialogue they create. While the question about the use of atomic bomb may never be settled, the question of the significance of the history is evident in both historical outcomes and current policy debates.

Chapter 2: What Is the History to Be Remembered?

Preserving History, Local and Global

As significant as its world-changing history is, Los Alamos and the surrounding area have many layers of history that run deeper than the twentieth-century. Petroglyphs, pottery sherds, and obsidian flakes show evidence of human occupation dating from the twelfth-century, with indigenous presence for millennia. Ancestral Pueblo sites saturate the landscape at Bandelier, Puye, Tsirege, Tsiping, and Tsankawi. Native peoples lived atop mesas or in cliff dwellings, growing corn, beans, and squash as staples. The Pajarito Plateau itself had permanent residents until approximately the sixteenth-century, when lack of water caused people to move to the nearby Rio Grande. The descendants of these ancient peoples are today part of Ohkay Owingeh, Santa Clara, San Ildefonso, Pojoaque, Nambe, and Tesuque pueblos.[13]

It was not until the nineteenth-century that people once again frequented the Pajarito Plateau. First, Spanish herders made their way into and

---

[13] Los Alamos Scientific Laboratory, *Los Alamos: Beginning of an Era, 1943-1945* (Los Alamos: Los Alamos Historical Society, 2008), 9-11.

through the lush landscape of the Valle Grande, the caldera (the saucer left behind when a volcano collapses on itself) of the Jemez Mountains. During the 1880s, the space was used for maneuvers by soldiers from Fort Marcy, located in nearby Santa Fe. At the same time, homesteaders began settling the plateau, where more than 30 families completed the process of homesteading. Homesteaders received free land up to 160 acres from the federal government if they farmed and built a home on it. Without irrigation at such a high elevation, the growing season was short. However, homesteaders managed to grow pinto beans, wheat, corn, squash, peas, pumpkins, potatoes, and other vegetables. During the winter, most families departed from the colder weather of the high altitude to valley areas with extended family and schools for children, who helped with planting in the spring, tending to crops in summer, and harvesting in fall.[14]

During this era, many visitors came through nearby Frijoles Canyon. A retired judge and his wife established Ten Elders Ranch, whose guests included archaeologist Edgar L. Hewitt, journalist and author Charles Lummis, and naturalist founder of the Boy

---

[14] Los Alamos Scientific Laboratory, *Los Alamos: Beginning of an Era, 1943-1945* (Los Alamos: Los Alamos Historical Society, 2008), 9; Los Alamos Historical Society, Los Alamos County, and Fuller Lodge/Historic Districts Advisory Board, *Los Alamos Homestead Tour*, brochure, 2012.

Scout movement in America, Ernest Thompson Seton. Bandelier National Monument was created in 1916, and there was no road into the canyon until 1933. By 1939, with the completion by the Civilian Conservation Corps of a new lodge and visitor center, the old guest lodges were demolished. One visitor to the region during this time was J. Robert Oppenheimer, whose health needs brought him to New Mexico, including the Jemez Mountains, where he encountered the Los Alamos Ranch School.[15]

The Los Alamos Ranch School offered a classical education as well as preparation for outdoor living. In 1917, Ashley Pond opened the school on land owned by Harold H. Brook, an advanced agriculturist who had purchased his holdings from the family of Antonio Sanchez, the first homesteader on the Pajarito Plateau. The unpolluted environment away from urban areas was part of the school's appeal, as it helped students with respiratory problems and encouraged outdoor discipline and self-sufficiency. The Los Alamos Ranch Schools integrated with the Boy Scouts, even adopting the organization's uniforms. Activities included swimming, fishing, hunting, hiking, basketball, tennis, horseback riding, skating, skiing, woodwork, and music. With studies that incorporated Latin, geometry, art, and science, the school for boys aged

---

[15] Los Alamos Scientific Laboratory, *Los Alamos: Beginning of an Era, 1943-1945* (Los Alamos: Los Alamos Historical Society, 2008), 11-12, 14.

12 to 18 aimed to cultivate responsibility through both academic and physical development and ultimately to place students into elite eastern universities.[16]

This was the society, composed of an elite school and a few dozen homestead families, which existed atop the Pajarito Plateau when the Manhattan Project arrived. One year after the Japanese attack on Pearl Harbor, A. J. Connell received notice from the Secretary of War that the United States would soon take over the Ranch School property for use in the war effort. Therefore, school administrators cancelled the 1942 Christmas recess, and accelerated the curriculum to ensure that the boys completed the school year by February 1943. When the last graduates left the school, as bulldozers for laboratory construction were already at work, it became clear the twenty-seven buildings of the Ranch School were insufficient for the scale of the project ahead. Similarly, homestead families were now displaced through eminent domain by the same government that had granted the property to them.[17]

---

[16] Los Alamos Scientific Laboratory, *Los Alamos: Beginning of an Era, 1943-1945* (Los Alamos: Los Alamos Historical Society, 2008), 13; Los Alamos Historical Society, *History of the Los Alamos Ranch School*, accessed via http://www.losalamoshistory.org/school.htm on 4 January 2013.

[17] Los Alamos Scientific Laboratory, *Los Alamos:*

Project Y, Manhattan Engineer District, New Mexico, USA

Having learned that German scientists were working on building an atomic bomb, the United States military decided in 1942 to work toward the same. Though Americans were not fully aware of German progress, the U.S. military believed that this project, if successful, could bring WWII to an end. In December 1942, Enrico Fermi had led a group of scientists in Chicago in creating the world's first human-made nuclear chain reaction. Still, to turn their understanding of this principle and achievement into a weapon, they needed at least a year of more scientific research and technological advancements, even if they were intensely focused on such a mission.[18]

Perhaps the biggest challenge was to prepare the fissionable material for the bomb. A chain reaction occurs when neutrons bombard and split the nuclei of other atoms, causing further fission that is enough to sustain reaction. Fission was the key

---

Beginning of an Era, 1943-1945 (Los Alamos: Los Alamos Historical Society, 2008), 14-15; Los Alamos Historical Society, Los Alamos County, and Fuller Lodge/Historic Districts Advisory Board, *Los Alamos Homestead Tour*, brochure, 2012.

[18] Los Alamos Scientific Laboratory, *Los Alamos: Beginning of an Era, 1943-1945* (Los Alamos: Los Alamos Historical Society, 2008), 6-7.

process that defined the atomic bomb. Scientists at the time knew of at least one kind of uranium nucleus that would divide upon absorbing a neutron, which then released energy and more neutrons. However, almost all naturally occurring uranium was too heavy an isotope to fission when capturing neutrons, and thus it was not useful for building a bomb. Uranium-235, a lighter isotope that could indeed fission and thus be used in a potential bomb, composed only .7% of naturally occurring uranium. Thus, industrial facilities in Oak Ridge, Tennessee, were constructed in 1942 in order to separate U-235 from the heavier isotopes in naturally occurring uranium and to produce enriched uranium that contained more than the natural proportion of U-235. Still, obstacles remained: U-235 was so rare that there was not enough to create even a sample of enriched uranium to observe in a laboratory.[19]

A few years prior to the Manhattan Project, scientists at the University of California in Berkeley, had created plutonium, which is not a naturally occurring element. The much more abundant and heavier isotope of uranium could capture neutrons to make plutonium, which scientists also determined was also a fissionable element and could be developed into a weapon. The army built reactors in Oak Ridge, Tennessee, and Hanford, Washington, to

---

[19] Los Alamos Scientific Laboratory, *Los Alamos: Beginning of an Era, 1943-1945* (Los Alamos: Los Alamos Historical Society, 2008), 6-7.

produce the uranium-235 and the plutonium.[20] To catch and exceed the German nuclear efforts, American scientists wanted to move fast in studying the two elements, even though only extremely small quantities were available.

J. Robert Oppenheimer had an enormous task in front of him at the Los Alamos laboratory: to lead the team to conduct the research, develop the technology, and create and deploy the bomb all within the pressure and time constraints of war. The U.S. Army constructed the laboratory on the Pajarito Plateau, a long and narrow highland that extends from the mountain range along a caldera. A high-altitude volcanic bench at about 7,000 feet elevation surrounded by mountain peaks reaching 10,000 feet and filled with numerous species of trees, the plateau's steep canyon walls carved from volcanic ash and lava flows provided a great location for such a secretive project. Oppenheimer knew about the area from time spent at his summer cabin in the region. He enjoyed the surroundings. The plateau fit the site criteria for this top-secret national security project. As a publication by the laboratory later explained, "[1] the site had to have adequate housing for 30 scientists; [2] the land had to be owned by the government or easily acquired; [3] it had to be large enough and uninhabited so as to permit safe separation of sites for experiments; [4] easy control of access for security and safety reasons was necessary;

---

[20] Ibid.

[5] and the place had to have enough cleared land, free of timber, to locate additional buildings at once."[21]

Because it was surrounded by national forest and cheap grazing land with few private properties, and because it included the infrastructure and buildings of the Los Alamos Ranch School, the Pajarito Plateau met the military's criteria. However, before the Los Alamos Ranch School students had even left the area, the school's couple dozen or so buildings proved insufficient for housing what became a population of 300 for the project—1,500 including the construction crews. The military base, however, could not be called Los Alamos to help maintain security, and thus it acquired the nickname "the Hill." Beginning on 1 January 1943, the University of California operated the laboratory through a nonprofit contract with the U.S. Army Corps of Engineers Manhattan Engineer District. Though recruiting administrative and technical positions proved to be difficult because project information was incomplete and the location was remote, top scientists from various universities and laboratories around the country and world were attracted by the challenge and significance of the project.[22]

---

[21] Los Alamos Scientific Laboratory, *Los Alamos: Beginning of an Era, 1943-1945* (Los Alamos: Los Alamos Historical Society, 2008), 7, 9, 14.
[22] Los Alamos Scientific Laboratory, *Los Alamos: Beginning of an Era, 1943-1945* (Los Alamos: Los

Throughout the first half of 1943, hundreds of families made the journey, even though, for the sake of security, most spouses were unaware of the work that was being done by their partners. As the wife of one of project scientist wrote, "I felt akin to the pioneer women accompanying their husbands across uncharted plains westward, alert to dangers, resigned to the fact that they journeyed, for weal or woe, into the Unknown." It was a new experience for many of them, who felt their world change quickly. Oppenheimer himself captured the sentiment of many he recruited: "The notion of disappearing into the desert for an indeterminate period and under quasi-military auspices disturbed a good many scientists and the families of many more."

Dorothy McKibbin, the "gatekeeper" to Los Alamos, would receive the new arrivals at now-famous 109 East Palace Avenue in Santa Fe. She addressed concerns, comforted the weary, and arranged for them and their belongings to make it up the Hill.[23] The newcomers encountered a town that was something of a "frontier" in many ways. For one, its built environment was clearly designed to be temporary; quickly constructed, cheap buildings were strewn about the site without much planning. As one

---

Alamos Historical Society, 2008), 14, 17, 19.
[23] Los Alamos Scientific Laboratory, *Los Alamos: Beginning of an Era, 1943-1945* (Los Alamos: Los Alamos Historical Society, 2008), 19.

of the early residents observed, "It was difficult to locate any place on that sprawling mesa which had grown so rapidly and so haphazardly, without order or plan." Amidst this chaotic layout were the log and stone buildings of the Ranch School. The dining hall, Fuller Lodge, became a cafeteria, and the former masters' houses provided homes for the project's top administrators. These fine buildings soon became surrounded by hastily built roads, apartments, barracks, dormitories, and labs—all built in a rush to finish the war. It took decades for housing in Los Alamos to catch up with demand (some would argue it still has not!). Despite the aim of a world-class project, this frontier town had little other infrastructure, as well: one telephone line in 1943 (three by 1945), one mail box (in Santa Fe), no laundry or hospital services until 1944, and insufficient water for the boom-town.[24]

Yet, the community offered much in the way of social and cultural institutions. In the first year of the project, residents created a town council to advise the military administration. The army established a nursery school as well as a 12-grade school system. Concerts, theaters, and movies were part of the thirty recreational and cultural organizations formed during the war. All of this was situated within a beautiful landscape with the volcanic Jemez and towering

[24] Los Alamos Scientific Laboratory, *Los Alamos: Beginning of an Era, 1943-1945* (Los Alamos: Los Alamos Historical Society, 2008), 19, 21.

Sangre de Cristo mountains on either side of the expansive Española Valley. The landscape also helped keep the project a secret—although it was a landscape that residents were barred from describing in conversations or correspondence, for fear of giving away the location.[25]

The success of the project depended upon secrecy. A barbed wire fence with armed guards surrounded Los Alamos, and the town was cut off from the surrounding region. Those who worked for the laboratory were not allowed to travel more than 100 miles from Los Alamos. Rules prohibited them from personal contact with their relatives—even an unplanned encounter with a friend outside the project was supposed to be reported to security. Famous scientists used false names without disclosing their occupations. Driver licenses, vehicle registrations, bank accounts, income tax returns, insurance policies, and food and gas rations were all issued not to names but to numbers. All mail was received in one post office box in Santa Fe, and outgoing mail was censored. Such tight regulation took its toll, as one resident recounted, "I couldn't write a letter without seeing a censor poring over it. I couldn't go to Santa Fe without being aware of hidden eyes upon me, watching, waiting to pounce on that inevitable misstep. It wasn't a pleasant feeling." This quest for

---

[25] Los Alamos Scientific Laboratory, *Los Alamos: Beginning of an Era, 1943-1945* (Los Alamos: Los Alamos Historical Society, 2008), 21-22.

uncompromised secrecy affected not just lifestyles but work, too. The military attempted to compartmentalize the scientific departments and projects in order to avoid anyone knowing of the whole project. However, Oppenheimer insisted on collaboration and instituted it through weekly colloquia.[26]

With collaboration, many elements of the project came together into two phases: first, research in physics, chemistry, and metallurgy; second, technology advancement into engineering ordnance design. Although the latter stage was originally planned to include military commissioning of the scientists, they remained civilians, unless they joined the laboratory staff through the Army's Special Engineer Detachment (SED). Between 1943 and 1945, the number of laboratory personnel multiplied ten-fold from 250 to 2,500 (half of them from the military, primarily SEDs). Regarding the atmosphere within this group, Oppenheimer observed, "Almost everyone knew that this job, if it were achieved, would be part of history. This sense of excitement, of devotion, and of patriotism, in the end, prevailed." This team focused first and foremost on scientific research, which later produced the hardware that changed the world. However, the labor put into bomb

---

[26] Los Alamos Scientific Laboratory, *Los Alamos: Beginning of an Era, 1943-1945* (Los Alamos: Los Alamos Historical Society, 2008), 22.

technology was far less than the effort directed toward overall nuclear science.[27]

Just over two years after the first scientists had arrived in Los Alamos, the project achieved the world's first manmade atomic blast with the successful test detonation on 16 July 1945 at the Trinity Site near Alamogordo, New Mexico. Three weeks later, the United States dropped an atomic bomb on the city of Hiroshima in Japan; and three days after that, on Nagasaki. Japan surrendered five days later. Manhattan Project had accomplished its mission: to end the war.[28]

With the revelation of the work that had occurred in Los Alamos, the local history of the Pajarito Plateau became global. Soon after the war, residents recognized the histories' many layers and interconnectedness in their early efforts. In 1966, the Atomic Energy Commission (AEC), the federal agency that managed nuclear energy, considered demolishing Fuller Lodge, which had recently ended its use as a hotel. Residents voiced their concern for the building, designed by influential architect John Gaw Meem, and the AEC appointed a committee to

---

[27] Los Alamos Scientific Laboratory, *Los Alamos: Beginning of an Era, 1943-1945* (Los Alamos: Los Alamos Historical Society, 2008), 22, 28.
[28] Los Alamos Scientific Laboratory, *Los Alamos: Beginning of an Era, 1943-1945* (Los Alamos: Los Alamos Historical Society, 2008), 23, 61.

gather opinions from the community. Fuller Lodge was saved. Most people hoped to see it operate as a cultural center or museum.[29]

With the approaching silver anniversary of the laboratory in 1967, the local chapter of the American Association of University Women created an organizing committee to explore the possibility of establishing a local historical society. The group turned to the president of the Historical Society of New Mexico for advice. During a speech in Fuller Lodge, Dr. Victor Westphall encouraged his audience by appealing to a sense of obligation, as he understood the global significance of the local history. "We would be remiss in our duties as citizens were we to take no action in preserving this history now before it becomes lost in the corridors of time." In the summer of 1967, local residents gathered on the patio of the Fuller Lodge to exchange stories that were up to a quarter-century old and to discuss the business of forming this incipient organization. They adopted by-laws and appointed officers to produce a charter. By September, the Los Alamos Historical Society held its charter meeting in Fuller Lodge.[30]

----

[29] Mary C. Byers, "In the Beginning," *History of the Los Alamos Historical Society and Museum, 1968-1988* (Los Alamos: Los Alamos Historical Society, May 1988), 1.
[30] Mary C. Byers, "In the Beginning," *History of the Los Alamos Historical Society and Museum, 1968-1988* (Los Alamos: Los Alamos Historical Society, May 1988), 1.

The society's first major project was to establish a museum as a tangible core for the organization. The former infirmary and later Guest Cottage, built prior to 1918, was the oldest extant building of the Ranch School, and it was located next to the Fuller Lodge. Its history extended into the Manhattan Project, too, as many visiting scientists as well as General Leslie R. Groves, the military director of the Manhattan Project, had stayed there. By 1968, the Los Alamos Historical Society gained use of the Guest Cottage as a museum. Volunteers focused on many projects, including conducting oral history interviews and gathering artifacts and materials, such as the locally relevant papers of John Gaw Meem, the architect of the Fuller Lodge, which soon became a National Historic Landmark. Meem provided the documents for the members of the Los Alamos Historical society to duplicate, and a formal effort began to create archives. In the summer, the museum with its volunteer work force opened, to a "gratifying" crowd. By 1971, the museum hired its first employee.[31]

Early in the development of the Los Alamos Historical Society, the Manhattan Project did not dominate the area's history as one might expect so soon after the Second World War. During the mid-1970s, the organization published the first of what

---

[31] Mary C. Byers, "In the Beginning," *History of the Los Alamos Historical Society and Museum, 1968-1988* (Los Alamos: Los Alamos Historical Society, May 1988), 1-4.

would become dozens of books for decades to come. It was the result of a reunion of graduates from the Ranch School. The Society's emphasis on the war years began more than a decade into its existence. During the early 1980s, the museum acquired and installed the historic gateway to 109 East Palace Avenue that was originally located in Santa Fe and had served as the arrival point in Santa Fe for those who came to join the Manhattan Project. Nonetheless, the Historical Society did not drift into becoming one dimensional in its interpretation of the local history. For example, in the mid-1980s, it conducted a bus tour to Santa Fe for historic architecture, and it also created a scholarship awardable to a local high school student who wrote a research paper about the early years of Los Alamos. The Historical Society also initiated a focus on the local history of homesteading, such as restoring the 1913 Romero Cabin. As the president of the organization at the time explained, "Everyone stays away from the Manhattan Project because that's the lab. So they focus on the Ranch School because it was here when the lab came, and then they drift back to the aboriginal Indians and forget that the homesteaders were here. The Spanish Americans from the Valley homesteaded here and used the land at least seasonally for their sheep and cattle. The ranchers and homestead habitations were part of the reason that rich Chicago sportsmen established the Pajarito Club. That led to the Ranch School and Oppenheimer's knowledge of the area... I was interested in the totality of the experience here."[32]

Programming and professionalizing increased as the Historical Society's resources and historical focuses multiplied. Docents started an outreach program with hands-on history programs in schools, and the New Mexico Humanities Council funded traveling exhibits. People from three states came to the museum to attend a workshop co-sponsored by the Smithsonian Institution, and the New Mexico Association of Museums provided professional development in community and school relations through museum outreach. The American Association for State and Local History became involved in advising about archival preservation and collections management. The 1980s proved to be a major period of growth and diversification in the history of the central preservation organization in the community. Today, the Los Alamos Historical Society is in a similar process, with increased professional staff, museum hours, variety of programming, archival capacity, award-winning publications, community engagement, focus on organizational development, and international attention.[33]

---

[32] Lore Watt, "The Society Continues," *History of the Los Alamos Historical Society and Museum, 1968-1988* (Los Alamos: Los Alamos Historical Society, May 1988), 7, 9-13.

[33] Lore Watt, "The Society Continues," *History of the Los Alamos Historical Society and Museum, 1968-1988* (Los Alamos: Los Alamos Historical Society, May 1988), 11-13.

Chapter 3: What Does It Mean to Remember?

After more than a decade of effort to create Manhattan Project National Historical Park before it even reached the congressional level, the United States in 2015 added to its cherished National Park Service units a new park that would span across the country in three states. In Los Alamos, as the chief laboratory facility of the Manhattan Project, the remembrance emphasized local experiences in interpretation, scope, and audience. However, this new type of historic site presents a heritage both local and international. With the introduction of the national park proposal, larger questions arise when remembering and interpreting a broader story to wider audiences, as the story becomes one of multi-national exchange. Yet, adding a global lens did not shift public attention away from the local construction of heritage; it intensified the contested effort to craft the local and regional history that would be projected to the world.

The Santa Fe New Mexican, the oldest daily newspaper west of the Mississippi River, was one forum in which local voices exchanged interpretations about the meaning of a park focused on the creation of the world's first atomic weapons. U.S. Senator Jeff Bingaman, representing New Mexico, championed the bill to establish the national park before he left office, because he described the Manhattan Project as "one of the most important events in our nation's history." Nevertheless, the newspaper based in New Mexico's capital city published an editorial that opposed the establishment of "a national park in honor of the atomic bomb" due to the destructive legacy of nuclear weapons. "Historic preservation is a Northern New Mexican hallmark, and Santa Fe's reputation in carrying it out has lots to do with our community's popularity as a place to visit," the *New Mexican* acknowledged, and "given our 400-year history, there has been plenty to preserve and commemorate; scenes grand and humble, public and private, civilian and military." Moreover, the periodical recognized, "There's no denying the importance of the Manhattan Project—and if it saved so much as one American life among the many that surely would have been lost if we'd invaded the Japanese mainland in 1945, we applaud its original goal." However, New Mexico's tradition of historic preservation and the importance of the Manhattan Project did not persuade the newspaper's editorial board to support the establishment of the national park, because "it brought instant death and long-term suffering to tens of thousands of Japanese civilians. And it opened a Pandora's box of evil in the wrong hands, where some soon landed—or maybe even in the right ones; nearly seven decades of global undiplomacy, and conventional wars touted as better than nuclear ones, are only part of the project's horrific legacy." Pointing to "anti-nuke activists around here" and to "opponents to development of nuclear anything, especially bombs," the *New*

Mexican predicted a "vast public relations challenge facing the national park proposal."[34]

The newspaper contended that the park was unnecessary. First, while indeed Gettysburg, Pearl Harbor, and Ford's Theater were incorporated into the National Park Service system, "folks interested in the Manhattan Project already may visit the excellent Bradbury Museum," located in Los Alamos and run by the Los Alamos National Laboratory. Second, with a weak economy and a federal government that had "warred and tax-cut its way to the brink of financial disaster, if not further," there was "no money" for a new project, especially when many national parks were "down-at-the-heels." Instead of spending scarce money on a new national park that seemed redundant with the Bradbury Science Museum, the periodical advocated for such money to be spent on maintaining the parks already in the system.[35]

David Simon, the former director of New Mexico State Parks and the former Southwest Regional Director of the National Parks Conservation Association, wrote a published rebuttal to the editorial that described the *New Mexican*'s position as "the wrong, short-term view" even as it gave credit to the newspaper as a "proven, steadfast defender of national parks and the environment." While the

---

[34] The New Mexican, "Manhattan Project Park Should Be Shelved," *The Santa Fe New Mexican*, 24 July 2011.
[35] Ibid.

Manhattan Project National Historical Park "involves difficult and painful subjects," Simon argued, "the park is absolutely necessary." A resident of New Mexico, Simon maintained, "America needs the National Park System to tell the full story of our history and heritage; it's also part of living our First Amendment principles, which value honest and open public dialogue about our nation." By protecting "key remaining places" and interpreting "irreplaceable historical resources," Simon believed that the "history objectively taught" would allow visiting audiences to "apply their own value systems and form their own opinions." The National Park Service was the right steward, because of its many units remembering controversial topics, such as the Civil War, slavery, the civil rights movement, treatment of American Indians, and Japanese internment. Specifically, in the Second World War, "far more American lives were saved in World War II due to the Manhattan Project than were tragically lost in the battles" commemorated by World War II Valor in the Pacific National Monument, War in the Pacific National Historical Park, and the Aleutian World War Two National Historic Area.[36]

Simon demonstrated that establishing this new park in such a context was critical. With the Manhattan Project recognized as "one of the most important events in world history," he observed that

---

[36] Dave Simon, "Manhattan Project National Park Is Controversial, but Necessary," *The Santa Fe New Mexican*, 30 July 2011.

the United States "can't afford to not establish this park," as it would risk the park system having "a gaping hole in its representation of some of the most significant U.S. historical themes." Pointing out that many state and national parks had been established during the Great Depression, Simon remained confident that funds could be appropriated from the "massive budgets" of the Departments of Energy and Defense, especially as the National Park Service approached its centennial in 2016.[*] "If done properly," Simon reasoned, "a Manhattan Project National Historical Park will take its place among the best National Park sites that commemorate epic national and world-changing events, present history objectively, and make us think—insisting that we inquire about ourselves as a country and as human beings." New Mexico had played a "key role" in an event that "changed the course of world history," and it was possible to "honor this history, while still debating the subjects that surround the bomb." In fact, "one can lament Truman's use of nuclear weapons, favor nuclear disarmament, and oppose nuclear energy yet still see the need for a Manhattan Project NPS unit." In short, the proposed park would not

---

[*] Supporters later argued that preserving and managing the sites of the proposed Manhattan Project National Historical Park was far less expensive than demolition; five years of NPS stewardship would cost $21 million, but proper demolition would cost $200 million, see William J. Broad, "Bid to Preserve Manhattan Project Sites in a Park Stirs Debate," *The New York Times*, 3 December 2012.

glorify nuclear weapons, but instead it would present an influential history and allow opportunities for more informed discussion about issues today that originate from this history.[37]

The contest over local heritage had implications about national remembrance and even perhaps notions of nationalism. With support in the United States by Congress and by the presidential administration, the Manhattan Project National Historical Park's potential meanings caught the attention of officials in Japan. In letters written to the United States, representatives of the cities of Hiroshima and Nagasaki requested that the potential park consider providing information about the damage caused by the bombings that resulted from the Manhattan Project. Hiroshima Mayor Kazumi Matsui indicated that "the people of Hiroshima were profoundly alarmed" by the proposal, and planning a park about a project that led to such destructive weapons was not in line with "the wishes of the millions of people around the world calling for the abolition of nuclear weapons... Such a park would communicate an erroneous and dangerous message to future generations." Consideration of current political aims affected the conceptualization and the interpretations of the Manhattan Project National Historical Park even before it existed. Nagasaki

---

[37] Dave Simon, "Manhattan Project National Park Is Controversial, but Necessary," *The Santa Fe New Mexican*, 30 July 2011.

Mayor Tomihisa Taue went further and urged the U.S. to take steps toward the promise made by Barack Obama in 2009 to seek a world without nuclear weapons.[38]

The various visions of the Manhattan Project National Historical Park triggered an exchange between nations, and it became an issue of diplomacy when Japanese leaders highlighted issues of historical memory and contemporary politics. Hence, it forced the United States to respond by clarifying the intent of the new national park. John Roos, the U.S. Ambassador to Japan, explained to the mayors of Hiroshima and Nagasaki that the national park would commemorate the activities during the war in a manner "reflective, rather than celebratory." He anticipated it as an "educational and commemorative facility." Roos addressed the call for Obama to fulfill his promise in nuclear policy, too, linking the present to the past as Matsui had done. He claimed, "As we look to the future and a world without nuclear weapons, it is fitting to remember that era through the lens of history, which the proposed park aims to

---

[38] "Hiroshima, Nagasaki Concerned Manhattan," *House of Japan*, 3 December 2011, http://www.houseofjapan.com/local/hiroshima-nagasaki-concerned-manhattan . David Barna, "Mainichi Daily News (Tokyo): Hiroshima, Nagasaki Express Concern about Manhattan Project Plan," http://webmail.itc.nps.gov/pipermail/infozone/2011-December/001727.html .

achieve." Echoing a similar reasoning, Cindy Kelly, president of the Atomic Heritage Foundation, maintained, "A national park site would deepen public understanding of the development of the atom bomb in the context of the time, including how its creators felt about it from a moral and personal perspective. It also will provide insight into an undertaking that transformed American science, politics, economics, society and culture and left an indelible legacy for the world today."[39]

The Atomic Heritage Foundation (AHF), an organization dedicated to preserving and interpreting the Manhattan Project and the Atomic Age, understood what became an international concern. Its newsletter reported on the explanation the U.S. ambassador had provided and stated, "The Park will serve as an educational tool and will consider the history of nuclear weapons from every angle." Consequently, the park would not be a site of celebration but rather one of education, provocation, and discussion—perhaps even debate. "With its long-standing oversight of controversial landmarks," such

---

[39] "US Tells Hiroshima Manhattan Project Park Plan Not Celebratory," *House of Japan*, 25 January 2012, http://www.houseofjapan.com/local/us-tells-hiroshima-manhattan-project-park-plan-not-celebratory ; "Roos Says A-Bomb Park Reflective, Not Celebratory," *The Japan Times*, 25 January 2012; Julian Ryall, "US Forced to Defend Manhattan Project Park to Japan," *The Telegraph*, 25 January 2012.

as Manzanar National Historic Site and Little Bighorn Battlefield, "the NPS is well practiced in telling the story of sites with divisive histories." AHF emphasized that the Department of Interior and the Department of Energy, both involved with the proposed park, "stand firmly behind" it. The Director of the National Park Service, Jonathan Jarvis, had already affirmed months earlier, "The National Park Service will be proud to interpret these Manhattan Project sites and unlock their stories in the years ahead." Secretary of Interior Ken Salazar had also proclaimed support by stating, "The secret development of the atomic bomb in multiple locations across the United States is an important story and one of the most transformative events in our nation's history. The Manhattan Project ushered in the atomic age, changed the role of the United States in the world community, and set the stage for the Cold War." Accordingly, the AHF expressed its trust, "Given the NPS's established experience with interpreting historical landmarks, the Atomic Heritage Foundation is confident the Park will do an excellent job informing the public about the history of the Manhattan Project and the Atomic Age for many generations to come."[40]

---

[40] "U.S. Ambassador to Japan Defends MP National Historical Park," Atomic Heritage Foundation, 25 January 2012, http://www.atomicheritage.org/index.php/ahf-updates-mainmenu-153/628-us-ambassador-to-japan-defends-manhattan-project-national-historical-park.html .

Preservation of these sites for future generations was at the heart of the effort—and opposition—to create the Manhattan Project National Historical Park. "Too often in this country, where we tend to look forward rather than back, by the time we decide a site is historic enough to make it worth preserving, a shopping mall has taken its place," remarked an opinion published in *Newsday*, a newspaper serving the New York City area. The bill must "pass soon, before time does what the developers haven't." While the article acknowledged the arguments that would surround "the propriety of preserving the crucible for the creation of man's greatest weapon of mass destruction," it maintained, "There is nothing to be gained by trying to erase, rewrite or sugarcoat history—not if we are going to learn from it." This rationale was why the National Trust for Historic Preservation supported the legislation establishing the Manhattan Project National Historical Park. After emphasizing that "the creation and use of the atomic bomb, developed by the Project's scientists, brought an end to World War II, altering the position of the United States in the world community while setting the stage for the Cold War," the organization urged its constituents and other audiences to contact federal legislators to ask them to support the bill: "The Manhattan Project is part of the National Trust's portfolio of National Treasures, and we are leading efforts to ensure this legislation is enacted. But we need your help to make it happen!"[41]

_____

[41] Dale McFeatters, "McFeatters: Turn Manhattan Project

59

The public attention and exposure of the proposed Manhattan Project National Historical Park continued to intensify and increase during the summer, as the legislation appeared ready to be brought to the floor of the House of Representatives. CBS highlighted it on national television on the 67th anniversary of the bombing of Hiroshima. In the program, Ellen McGehee, historic buildings manager at Los Alamos National Laboratory, emphasized the importance of preservation: "You really can't understand how the scientists were working and what conditions they were working under unless you come out to the place where history really happened." Susan Gordon, representing the Alliance for Nuclear Accountability, expressed a reaction "of caution." According to the CBS reporter, "While she agrees what scientists accomplished here is worthy of a national park, she worries commemorating the bomb may celebrate it, too, glossing over the problem of nuclear waste." On camera, Gordon contended, "It needs to be a much more balanced approach that addresses the environmental and health consequences of the production of nuclear weapons in this country."

Sites into National Parks," *Newsday*, 3 August 2012; Amy Cole, "The Manhattan Project: 20th Century History, 21st Century Significance," *PreservationNation Blog*, National Trust for Historic Preservation, 19 July 2012, http://blog.preservationnation.org/2012/07/19/the-manhattan-project-20th-century-history-21st-century-significance/#.UP5dzq6Oivg .

McGehee, when directed by the reporter to the "sobering effect of what was being built and designed," responded, "History isn't always pretty, and I think it's important that we don't lose this history, or lose the ability to reflect on that history."[42] For both perspectives presented about the potential national park, historic preservation was a means for history, legacy, and current-day reflection.

After much public coverage and debate at local, national, and international levels, a congressional vote on the park legislation became imminent during the late summer of 2012. In August, *The Washington Post* took an unusually rare action by publishing an editorial about a specific piece of legislation on a subject other than major national policies like Social Security or health care. "A bipartisan initiative seeks" to add this new unit to the National Park Service, the newspaper stated, and it endorsed this proposed park: "That's a fine idea." The editorial contended, "Such a move would expand access to these crucial historical sites as well as provide funding and staffing to preserve them. Given their importance in the history of the United States, the Cold War and the 20th century, Congress should pass the park designation bill by Sen. Jeff Bingaman (D-N.M.) and companion legislation by Rep. Doc Hastings (R-Wash.)." The Manhattan Project "ranks among the most significant

---

[42] "Atomic Bomb Labs May Be Made a National Park," *CBS This Morning*, aired 6 August 2012, and available at http://www.cbsnews.com/video/watch/?id=7417292n .

chapters of the American Century," and it created "a weapon that changed the course of warfare forever." *The Washington Post* did recognize the challenge of interpreting such a site: "It will be a daunting task. The bill acknowledges that the project's legacy is 'significant, far-reaching and complex.' The Manhattan Project harnessed American scientific, engineering and industrial prowess in an effort that many saw as essential to the survival of the free world in its fight against fascism. But many of its participants wrestled within themselves then and afterward over their part in creating such a frightful tool of death." The editorial articulately framed larger historical questions with the challenge of modern presentation, "The decision to use the weapon, to destroy the Japanese cities of Hiroshima and Nagasaki, remains, and will always remain a question of keen historical debate. The explosions brought to a swift end a war that might otherwise have dragged on for a long time, at a cost of hundreds of thousands more lives, both American and Japanese. But they killed hundreds of thousands of Japanese civilians, both in August 1945 and subsequently from radiation poisoning. A successful exhibit will present the choice that President Harry S. Truman faced in all its complexity without seeking to decide the issues for visitors." With a challenge of interpreting not unlike that of Little Rock Central High School and the Manzanar site, the National Park Service has developed the "significant experience" needed to handle "fraught histories," according to the newspaper, and as a "seminal moment in world history," the Manhattan Project "surely warrants the wider audience this legislative push would bring."[43]

The next month, the bill to establish Manhattan Project National Historical Park failed in the House of Representatives on 20 September 2012. "Rarely does a proposed new national park run into this kind of opposition," the report published in the *Albuquerque Journal* read, "but this one deals with the A-bomb." Representative Dennis Kucinich, Democrat from Ohio, voiced the loudest opposition to the bill, as he disapproved of opportunities to "celebrate ingenuity that was used to put all humanity at risk." He placed his stance within the context of current political challenges: "At a time when we should be organizing the world toward abolishing nuclear weapons before they abolish us, we are instead indulging in admiration at our cleverness as a species." As he viewed the potential implication of the proposed national park, "The bomb is about graveyards; it's not about national parks." The newspaper report also featured the voice of the Atomic Heritage Foundation, which stated that the National Park Service would interpret the Manhattan Project "in all its complexity, giving voice to all sides of this contested history. It is important that we remember and reflect upon the past." Clearly, the legacy of nuclear weapons dominated the debate over the new national park, whether it was in a local forum a year earlier, national

---

[43] Editorial Board, "Commemorating the Bomb," *The Washington Post*, 12 August 2012.

news outlets, international diplomatic exchanges, or on the floor of Congress. So pervasive was this legacy in envisioning the park that even its proponents did not reject these themes but instead argued that the park allowed an opportunity to remember the impacts, highlight the legacies, and represent multiple viewpoints—among others.[44]

While the Manhattan Project National Historical Park won a majority of the vote in the House of Representatives, it failed to pass. The bill had come up during a "suspension of the rules," a procedure which is designed for non-controversial legislation and hence requires only forty minutes of debate. However, because this bill turned out more controversial than expected, the vote of 237-180 (about 55% to 42%) was not enough to pass, as a "suspension of the rules" requires a two-thirds majority. Representative Doc Hastings, Republican from Washington, sponsored the Manhattan Project National Historical Park Act (HR 5987), but 112 members of his own party voted against it, as did 68 Democrats. As a result, Representative Kucinich claimed to have led "a bipartisan coalition of 180

---

[44] Richard Simon, "A-Bomb Park Bill Fails in House," *Albuquerque Journal*, 22 September 2012; Richard Simon, "House Rejects Manhattan Project Park Bill," *Journal North*, 21 September 2012; Richard Simon, "U.S. House Effort to Recognize the Atomic Bomb with New National Park Is a Dud," *The Dallas Morning News*, 20 September 2012; Richard Simon, "House Effort to Recognize the A-Bomb Is a Dud," *Los Angeles Times*, 20 September 2012.

Members of Congress to stand for veterans, for fiscal responsibility [due to a lack of funds to maintain existing parks,] and friendship with the Japanese people."[45]

United for Peace and Justice, an organization promoting justice and peace in movements local and global, applauded Representative Kucinich's stand, driven by what the organization deemed an "inspiring testimony." The organization's website reported, he "led a successful bipartisan effort to defeat a bill in Congress that would have established a new national park celebrating the technological achievements of the Manhattan Project." The article quoted Kucinich, as he linked the commemoration of the technology with the impacts and legacies that technology created: "The technology which created the bomb cannot be separated from the horror the bomb created… If there was going to be a new park, it should serve as a solemn monument to Japanese American friendship that rose from the ashes and the worldwide work for nuclear disarmament that continues to this day, rather than a celebration of a technology that has brought such destruction to the world. Failure to recognize this dimension, even in its first iteration, really is a significant injustice." This was a considerable victory, as interpreted by United for Peace and Justice, because the legislation had the support of the Obama

---

[45] Randi Minetor, "Manhattan Project Park Bill Achieves Majority, but Fails in the House," *Examiner*, 21 September 2012.

administration. As Representative Kucinich explained, "The 'Bomb Park' is a mistake. We should not spend another $21,000,000 more to 'spike the nuclear football.' We are defined by what we celebrate. We should not celebrate nuclear bombs." Unlike the conception by National Park Service of its own units, Representative Kucinich understood the park, and perhaps national parks in general, as triumphant rather than remembrance, congratulatory rather than educational, monumental rather than preservationist.[46]

However, not all left-leaning media sources supported Kucinich's view. For example, the Huffington Post responded with a case for supporting the bill by Jim DiPeso, Policy Director of ConservAmerica, an organization "founded in 1995 to resurrect the GOP's great conservation tradition and to restore natural resource conservation and sound environmental protection as fundamental elements of the Republican Party's vision for America." DiPeso characterized Kucinich's position as "ideological posturing run amok," because

---

[46] Jackie Cabasso, "UFPJ Applauds Dennis Kucinich for Leading Defeat of Bill in U.S. House of Representatives to Establish Manhattan Project National Park," United for Peace and Justice, 16 October 2012, http://www.unitedforpeace.org/2012/10/16/ufpj-applauds-dennis-kucinich-for-leading-defeat-of-bill-in-u-s-house-of-representatives-to-establish-manhattan-project-national-park .

"national historical parks are opportunities for education. Kucinich's statement insulted the dedicated professionals in the National Park Service who responsibly interpret the events that shaped our country's history." The author's faith in the reputation and skill of the National Park Service was key to his argument, as it was for others who voiced support for the national park during the preceding fourteen months. "The historical significance of the Manhattan Project is beyond question," DiPeso observed, "and that is the essence of why Congress should authorize a national historical park to commemorate and interpret the project." His piece in the *Huffington Post* was clear in its claims, "Kucinich's personal views on the development and use of the atomic bomb are irrelevant to the project's importance to American history." The influence of the Manhattan Project went well beyond the United States as "a crash program" that shaped the outcome of "a global conflict in which the future of Western civilization hung in the balance." Consequently, in interpreting the Manhattan Project, its impacts, and its legacy, "the Park Service would be responsible for shedding light on this and the many other military, technological, geopolitical, and ethical dimensions of the Manhattan Project, even if the story tells people things they would rather not hear." Provocation was an important asset of this proposed park.[47]

---

[47] Jim DiPeso, "Pass the Bill Establishing Manhattan Project National Historical Park," *The Huffington Post*, 26 September 2012, http://www.huffingtonpost.com/jim-

Provoking people to think critically, however, did not mean that the National Park Service would take a side on the many issues tied to the Manhattan Project. The agency, DiPeso emphasized, is not "in the propaganda business, as Kucinich seems to believe." The NPS "has capably interpreted many of the difficult and tragic episodes in America's history that are commemorated at national parks and historical sites," such as slavery, racial segregation, the Trail of Tears, and Japanese internment. These sites dedicated to such difficult pasts provided opportunities for "modern Americans [to] come to grips with our history and reflect on the meaning of events that tell our country's story." While Kucinich's "perspective is worth hearing," DiPeso pointed out that it was "not the only voice that should be heard." He expressed his disapproval of politicians using history as a chance to attract political attention: "That's why we don't let congressmen handle historical interpretation in our national parks, a job they surely would corrupt with ideological posturing and bumper sticker politicking." In fact, politicians were an obstacle to understanding history, "Imagine the damage our national park system would suffer if we allowed ideologues to interfere with responsible interpretation of our history in order to conform to this or that notion of political correctness." Therefore, "Congress should pass the park authorizing

---

dipeso/manhattan-project-national-historical-park_b_1917059.html ; ConservAmerica homepage, http://conservamerica.org , accessed 14 January 2013.

legislation, then get out of the way and let the National Park Service do the interpretation job it does so well," DiPeso powerfully concluded.[48]

Based in Oak Ridge, Tennessee, location of one of the three proposed sites of the Manhattan Project National Historical Park, *The Oak Ridger* agreed with DiPeso's views. The newspaper published two prominent opinions that supported the park. Bill Wilcox, the Oak Ridge city historian, delivered a speech that had four main reasons for commemorating the Manhattan Project, according to the article's author, D. Ray Smith. First, Smith wrote, Wilcox clarified that "we are NOT celebrating the bombing of Hiroshima and Nagasaki," but rather the end of "this war that brought 54 million deaths." Second, stopping the war ceased the plans of a major invasion of Japan that "anticipated to bring an appalling 250,000 deaths of our men and millions of Japanese deaths." Third, the Manhattan Project ushered in the Nuclear Age, when the "tremendous energy of the atom was, for the first time, released and controlled." Finally, nuclear science and technology led to "highly beneficial applications," including nuclear medicine, commercial nuclear power, and applications in industry and agriculture

---

[48] Jim DiPeso, "Pass the Bill Establishing Manhattan Project National Historical Park," *The Huffington Post*, 26 September 2012, http://www.huffingtonpost.com/jim-dipeso/manhattan-project-national-historical-park_b_1917059.html .

that "improved the quality of life to mankind all over the world." Smith believed Wilcox had presented what would become "a classic in historic preservation literature," which concluded by highlighting that "the beginning of the end of war—is remembrance," and hence, "we do not remember our wartime roles in order to glorify that or any war, but to remember how terrible war really is and hopefully do something more to bring the world lasting peace." Therefore, even arguments favorable to the park were didactic, as they tried to address the moral high ground claimed by the opposition.[49]

In the same vein, Smith included a letter written to Representative Kucinich by Martin Skinner, who had worked for many years in physics, separating stable isotopes that had an impact on people's daily lives. As Skinner reasoned, "While the death toll was large as expected, it was nowhere equal to the loss if we had invaded Japan. Just look at how the Japanese defended the islands to almost the last man. The combined losses of Japan and the U.S. would have been tremendous. The men on ships in the Pacific headed for the invasion were told they likely would not return. Ask any of those men—some are still alive—how they felt when peace was declared!" Kucinich was mistaken, Skinner maintained, as the park would be "much more than the celebration of the

---

[49] D. Ray Smith, "Historically Speaking: Putting the Manhattan Project into Proper Perspective," *The Oak Ridger*, 8 October 2012.

bomb technology," as "what is to be celebrated is the ingenuity of scientists and engineers who have developed technologies that continue to benefit hundreds and thousands of people all over the world every day of the year." For example, "nuclear medicine is an outgrowth of the Manhattan Project, as is nuclear propulsion for space exploration." Skinner also mentioned that there were many sources for "information on the peaceful utilization of many aspects of nuclear technology."[50]

At the end of 2012, public attention on the Manhattan Project National Historical Park was revived with a renewed effort to include the park's establishment in the final wave of legislation of the 112th Congress. *The New York Times* captured the essence of the continuing disagreement about the potential park: "Critics have faulted the plan as celebrating a weapon of mass destruction, and have argued that the government should avoid that kind of advocacy. Historians and federal agencies reply that preservation does not imply moral endorsement, and that the remains of so monumental a project should be saved as a way to encourage comprehension and public discussion." When the Manhattan Project National Historical Park Act had failed in September 2012, Representative Doc Hastings, the sponsor of the bill, had not given up hope, as he stated, "While it

---

[50] D. Ray Smith, "Historically Speaking: Putting the Manhattan Project into Proper Perspective," *The Oak Ridger*, 8 October 2012.

didn't receive the supermajority needed to be sent to the Senate today, a big bipartisan majority of the House voted to establish the Manhattan Project National Historical Park. We've shown there is support for this park and will be working towards the goal of enacting this into law before the end of this year." As the Chairman of the House Natural Resources Committee, he tried to make this a reality.[51]

In this political moment, *The Boston Globe* declared, "The House shouldn't make the same mistake twice." As the second push for the park seemed to be underway, the newspaper published an editorial in support of the effort. The article acknowledged, "The Manhattan Project that created the first atomic bomb was a great success—and, in the eyes of many, a cautionary tale about the dangers of technological proliferation." However, the editorial understood that "the best way to forget such complicated lessons of the past is to pretend they never happened," something those in the House of Representatives who voted against the Manhattan Project National Historical Park Act "ought not to forget." The argument by Representative Kucinich was "shortsighted," *The Boston Globe* argued, because "many advances in science and technology

---

[51] William J. Broad, "Bid to Preserve Manhattan Project Sites in a Park Stirs Debate," *The New York Times*, 3 December 2012; Richard Simon, "U.S. House Effort to Recognize the Atomic Bomb with New National Park Is a Dud," *The Dallas Morning News*, 20 September 2012.

have deadly uses as well as peaceful ones, and sometimes the deadly ones help keep the peace." The newspaper brought up the oft-invoked point about the historical park's usefulness as a starting point for discussion about contemporary politics and ethics: "The questions that could be raised at the proposed Manhattan Project National Park are exactly the ethical quandaries that contemporary students—and lawmakers—should be confronting." To illustrate this point further, *The Boston Globe* pointed to an interview of Heather McClenahan, Executive Director of the Los Alamos Historical Society, which aired on National Public Radio earlier in the week. McClenahan articulated some of these issues: "Why did we do this? What were the good things that happened? What were the bad? How do we learn lessons from the past? How do we not ever have to use an atomic bomb in warfare again?" Indeed, this historical site would have a tremendous relevancy for teaching leaders and citizens today.[52]

Thanks to the politics and ethics of nuclear weapons, the memory of the impact of the atomic bomb on the Second World War and its aftermath

---

[52] Editorial Board, "Manhattan Project National Park Would Commemorate History, Not Glorify It," *The Boston Globe*, 7 December 2012; Ted Robbins, "Manhattan Project Sites Part of Proposed Park," National Public Radio, 4 December 2012, transcript, http://www.npr.org/templates/transcript/transcript.php?storyId=166402093 .

continued to be contested, even outside of the debate surrounding the Manhattan Project National Historical Park. "Two foundational beliefs have colored our views of nuclear weapons since the end of World War 2," Ashutosh Jogalekar, a chemist with interest in the history of science, wrote in the *Scientific American*: "One, that they were essential to or at least very significant for ending the war, and two, that they have been and will continue to be linchpins of deterrence." However, he pointed to a new book, *Five Myths about Nuclear Weapons*, which "demolish[es] these and other myths about nukes." According to Jogalekar's account of the book, the myth of nuclear weapons being paramount to ending the war perpetuated by "post facto rationalization" constructs a narrative that "brilliant scientists worked on a fearsome weapon in a race against the Nazis, and when the Nazis were defeated, handed it over to world leaders who used it to bring a swift end to a most horrible conflict. Psychologically it fits into a satisfying and noble narrative." Yet, it doesn't take "'revisionist' history," as Jogalekar saw it, to realize that declassified files in American, Soviet, Japanese, and British archives allow "us to piece together the cold facts and reveal what exactly was the impact of the atomic bombings of Japan on the Japanese decision to end the war. They tell a story very different from the standard narrative." These documents, he contended, uncover that the atomic bombings caused only "mild consternation" among Japanese leaders, while the declaration of war and the invasion of Manchuria and the Sakhalin Islands by the Soviet Union had "a very significant impact" and caused "the same men" to become "extremely rattled."[53]

Jogalekar also addressed the second most popular "myth" of the five major "myths" covered in the book. As he recounted it, "Conventional thinking continues to hold that the Cold War stayed cold because of nuclear weapons." While this was "true to some extent," he admitted, "what it fails to recognize is how many times the war threatened to turn hot." For example, the Cuban Missile Crisis represented one of the "near-hits that could have easily led to nuclear war," as we learned more about these events with increasing research through the growing number of declassified documents. During the Cuban Missile Crisis, for instance, Kennedy chose to impose a blockade on Cuba, despite the fact that Soviets "had made it clear that any action against Cuba would provoke war," and "so deterrence does not seem to have worked" in this case. Moreover, the argument for deterrence overlooks "normal accidents," Jogalekar mentioned, due to "miscalculation, misunderstandings or paranoia. The fact is that these weapons of mass destruction have a life of their own; they are beyond the abilities of human beings to completely harness because human weaknesses and flaws also have lives of their own." These

---

[53] Ashutosh Jogalekar, "On the Uselessness of Nuclear Weapons," *Scientific American*, 13 January 2013; Ward Wilson, *Five Myths About Nuclear Weapons* (New York: Houghton Mifflin Harcourt, 2013).

considerations helped Jogalekar believe that some of the purported positive effects of nuclear weapons were, in fact, rationalizations for their continued production and possession.[54]

Acknowledging what seemed like mythology would change the future, Jogalekar reasoned. "If we realize that the atomic bombing of Hiroshima and the general destruction of cities played little role in ending World War 2," he surmised, "almost everything that we think we know about the power of nuclear questions is called into question." Therefore, nuclear weapons have remained like "a giant T. rex; one could possibly imagine a use for such a creature in extreme situations, but by and large it serves as an unduly sensitive and enormously destructive creature whose powers are waiting to be unleashed on to the world." Consequently, Jogalekar reckoned, "Having the beast around is just not worth its supposed benefits anymore, especially when most of these benefits are only perceived and have been extrapolated from a sample size of one." In fact, he asserted, these were "outdated weapons," because "experts have pointed out since the 1980s that technology and computational capabilities have now improved to an extent that allows conventional precision weapons to do almost all the jobs that were once imagined for nuclear weapons; the U.S. especially now has enough conventional firepower to protect itself and to overpower almost any nuclear-

---

[54] Ibid.

armed state with massive retaliation." As a result, he stressed, "The fact is that nuclear weapons as an instrument of military policy are now almost completely outdated even from a technical standpoint." Unfortunately, as Jogalekar lamented, "We continue to nurture this creature," but still, "much progress has been made in reducing the nuclear arsenals of the two Cold War superpowers, but others have picked up the slack and continued to pursue the image and status—and not actual fighting capacity—they think nuclear weapons confer on them." Iran and its nuclear program, highlighted early in the opening chapter, could fit such a description, and it certainly had heavy consequences, both globally and domestically in the United States, particularly during the 2012 election cycle.[55]

With all of these ongoing public discourses, remembering nuclear history remains a challenge, as it is fraught with political and ethical implications, regardless of how it is interpreted even within a historical lens. Not surprisingly, the Manhattan Project National Historical Park both reflects these powerful feelings and also helps trigger them further. The stories of pain and triumph could simultaneously justify and invalidate the creation of a national park focused on the world's first nuclear weapons—the key is in the interpretation of the histories at these sites, and the view one takes of what opportunities they provide (i.e. celebration versus reflection). Either

---

[55] Ibid.

way, the modern implications cannot be escaped, as demonstrated by voices advocating and opposing the Manhattan Project National Historical Park. These contested narratives and powerful reactions, regardless of the particular position, substantiate the relevance of the national park. The debate over its establishment became a forum for grappling with the meanings of remembering the Manhattan Project, the influential histories of the sites, and its legacies that still today profoundly shape common rhetoric, foreign policy, and energy solutions. It is a past that still thrives in the present and decidedly helps mold the future—the Manhattan Project National Historical Park could bring all this together as a space that provokes conversation otherwise unlikely between citizens in today's insularity created by our polarized political climate.

Chapter 4: How to Remember?

Much of the debate surrounding the legitimacy of the Manhattan Project National Historical Park focused on the ethical questions of whether using nuclear weapons on Japan was morally justified and strategically necessary to end the Second World War. These underlying questions will never have definitive answers, and thus, historians and the public will likely never reach a consensus. More importantly, possible answers to these questions are distractions from the central concern in discussing the creation of the park: whether Manhattan Project sites are worthy of preservation, and whether the National Park Service is the appropriate steward. The frame of conversation must move away from counter-factual assumptions and assertions about the use (or avoidance) of the atomic bomb in history, and it must focus instead on the question of the significance of the history that unfolded.

One consistent measuring tool for historic significance is the National Register of Historic Places. William Murtagh, the first Keeper of the National Register of Historic Places, identified it "as the major vehicle to identify cultural resources." Of the Register's four major criteria for evaluation (event, person, design/construction, and information potential), the Manhattan Project meets all four. The globally transformative event is certainly, as Criterion A requires, "associated with events that have made a significant contribution to the broad patterns of our history." With the involvement of some of the top scientists in the world led by J. Robert Oppenheimer, the Manhattan Project is also, as Criterion B prescribes, "associated with the lives of significant persons in our past." This team coming together for this event that led to the capstone development of the world's first nuclear bombs "represent the work of a master" as Criterion C dictates. Although the presence of active laboratory facilities on and near many of the historic sites associated with the Manhattan Project prevents thorough archaeological investigation today, these historic locations are still "likely to yield, information important in history," as Criterion D stipulates. Therefore, it is not surprising that some sites related to the Manhattan Project in Los Alamos were approved for National Historic Landmark status as early as 1965. The significance of the Manhattan Project has long been recognized. In fact, the degree and content of the arguments of the park's opponents proves its historic importance.[56]

---

[56] William J. Murtagh, *Keeping Time: The History and Theory of Preservation in America* (New York: Sterling Publishing Co., 1988), 169; *How to Apply the National Register Criteria for Evaluation*, National Register Bulletin 15, National Park Service, Department of the Interior, accessed on 1 March 2013 via http://www.nps.gov/history/nr/publications/bulletins/nrb15 / ; *National Historic Landmarks Survey*, National Park Service, accessed on 1 March 2013 via http://www.nps.gov/nhl/designations/Lists/NM01.pdf .

With the significance of the Manhattan Project unquestioned by any side, it is important to then establish what role historic preservation plays by protecting such a painful yet triumphant history. Geographer David Lowenthal points toward a nuanced understanding of the process of constructing historical memory: "Benign and baneful consequences are intertwined; heritage vice is inseparable from heritage virtue. Yet heritage is customarily either admired or reviled in toto. Devotees ignore or slight its threats; detractors simply damn its ills and deny its virtues." Art historians Robert Nelson and Margaret Olin contend for the same complexity: "Monuments enjoy multiple social roles," as they are "not merely cold, hard, and permanent," but are also "living, vital, immediate, and accessible." Nelson and Olin argue, "A monument can achieve a powerful symbolic agency... attacking a monument threatens a society's sense of itself and its past." The Manhattan Project National Historical Park is not simply about the past, but it is about the present, just like any creation of heritage. As Nelson and Olin maintain, a "monument does not privilege the past at the expense of the present." Such an awareness of the present triggered by the Manhattan Project National Historical Park would include the viewpoints expressed by those who disapprove of the legacy of nuclear weapons. As Nelson and Olin explain, "Monuments are important, because people want to see them, and when that quest is realized actually or virtually, monuments become social agents." Thoughtful and provocative interpretation at the Manhattan Project National

Historical Park could uproot a visitor's simplistic understanding of all things nuclear. The experience of a monument, Nelson and Olin claim, "remakes the memories of individuals and connects both object and beholder to larger social structures." Therefore, obstructing the creation of this type of monument, according to Nelson and Olin, "constitutes a powerful and communal violation." Any attempt "to redirect cultural memory" would mean losing the contemporary educational opportunities about all perspectives on the historical impact of this transformative technology that remain possible only through site-specific learning, As Nelson and Olin highlight, "memory and monument are to each other as process and product."[57]

The field of historic preservation in the postmodern world has extensively dealt with conflicted histories and has developed the tools for properly handling complex stories. Jennifer McStotts, a scholar of historic preservation and urban studies, points out, "Modern preservation values are

---

[57] David Lowenthal, "The Heritage Crusade and Its Contradictions," in Max Page and Randall Mason, eds., *Giving Preservation a History: Histories of Historic Preservation in the United States* (New York: Routledge, 2004), 21; Robert S. Nelson and Margaret Olin, "Introduction," in Robert S. Nelson and Margaret Olin, eds., *Monuments and Memory, Made and Unmade* (Chicago: University of Chicago Press, 2003), 3, 6, 5, 6, 3-4, 4.

broadening to include sites with contested histories." She discerns that "this development represents the latest stage of the American preservation movement and an inclusion of values from reverence of history and historic sites to the desire for a contemplative, authentic experience." J. E. Tunbridge and G. J. Ashworth, who study heritage tourism, reason that because "history is created to serve contemporary functions," it follows that "the creation of a national heritage" becomes "a matter of policy." The establishment by the national government of a National Park Service unit dedicated to the key sites of the Manhattan Project, with its functions in the present drawn from the past, would fit just such a policy. As McStotts maintains, "Endurance of these landscapes is necessary for healing and for remembrance of the meaning and significance of the associated experience."[58]

---

[58] Jennifer McStotts, "Preserving Walls: Cultural Landscapes with Divisive Histories," Cari Goetcheus and Eric MacDonald, eds., *Exploring the Boundaries of Historic Landscape Preservation*, Proceedings of the Twenty-ninth Annual Meeting of the Alliance for Historic Landscape Preservation 2007 (Clemson: Clemson University Digital Press, 2008), 113, 114; J. E. Tunbridge and G. J. Ashworth, *Dissonant Heritage: The Management of the Past as a Resource in Conflict* (Chichester: John Wiley & Sons, 1996), 46; Jennifer McStotts, "Preserving Walls: Cultural Landscapes with Divisive Histories," Cari Goetcheus and Eric MacDonald, eds., *Exploring the Boundaries of Historic Landscape Preservation*, Proceedings of the Twenty-ninth Annual Meeting of the

Thus, the Manhattan Project National Historical Park could serve as precisely the poignant forum necessary to spark debate about the past and future policy. The park's opponents would cleanse historical memory and disallow discussions toward future policies. John Michael Vlach, professor of anthropology and American Studies who was involved with a controversial exhibit at the Library of Congress about African slavery in the United States, insists, "A controversial topic such as the history of slavery cannot be expected to move serenely through the public; as the stuff of difficult history, it is guaranteed to provoke a strong reaction. But if the passions that are stirred can be harnessed to a useful social project, such as preparation for a sustained struggle for social reform, then difficult history can fulfill the promise at which all scholars aim." Anthropologist Richard Flores observes, "Myth of history, cultural memory or public history, stories of the past track through us and over us as they provide narrative representations and public imaginaries that help us to make our way through the world." He reminds us that "forgetting is not a passive experience; like remembering, it is an active process that involves erasure." By failing to pass the legislation for the Manhattan Project National Historical Park, which would have preserved and interpreted perhaps the most significant event of the twentieth-century, the U.S. House of Representatives

Alliance for Historic Landscape Preservation 2007 (Clemson: Clemson University Digital Press, 2008), 113.

effectively attempted to erase this history from the official national memory.[59]

Instead, the National Park Service, which has proven its capability and willingness to interpret multiple perspectives about difficult histories, should be allowed to show a maturity by the United States about its history by confronting its past with all its complexities rather than wishful attempts of cleansing. Anthropologist Andrew Lass cautions that the "nation-state's concern for remembrance, or encoding, is paralleled only by its obsession with forgetting, or erasure." Having the courage to create the Manhattan Project National Historical Park would help the United States transcend this pattern and demonstrate responsibility about its past that continues to affect its present and future. Robert Bevan, who writes widely and frequently about architecture and design, warns against the destruction of the built environment as a destruction of memory, as he views "the destruction of the cultural artifacts of an enemy people or nation as a means of dominating, terrorizing, dividing or eradicating it altogether." By

---

[59] John Michael Vlach, "The Last Great Taboo Subject: Exhibiting Slavery at the Library of Congress," James Oliver Horton and Lois E. Horton, eds., *Slavery and Public History: The Tough Stuff of American Memory* (New York: The New Press, 2006), 72; Richard Flores, *Remembering the Alamo: Memory, Modernity, and the Master Symbol* (Austin: University of Texas Press, 2002), x, xv.

demonizing the Manhattan Project and the national park dedicated to it, opponents of the Manhattan Project National Historical Park have effectively created a historical enemy, which they wish to eradicate from national memory as a way of censuring it. Bevan goes so far as to call this practice "the pursuit of ethnic cleansing or genocide by other means, or the rewriting of history in the interests of a victor reinforcing his conquests." He explains, "That which is valued by a dominant culture or cultures in society is preserved and cared for: the rest can be mindlessly or purposefully destroyed, or just left to rot." The significance and impacts of the Manhattan Project must drive the dominant culture, expressed through the U.S. national government, to nurture the Manhattan Project National Historical Park, instead of intentionally omitting this critical story from the national narrative.[60]

For those opposed to all things nuclear in the present and future, the Manhattan Project National Historical Park does not diminish their perspective but rather offers a forum and opportunity to include and remember their voices. A poignant site for provoking reflection, contemplation, analysis,

---

[60] Andrew Lass, "Romantic Documents and Political Monuments: The Meaning-Fulfillment of History in 19th-Century Czech Nationalism," *American Ethnologist* 15 (3), 1988, p. 467; Robert Bevan, *The Destruction of Memory: Architecture at War* (London: Reaktion Books, 2006), 8, 11-12.

conversation, and debate about the merits of nuclear technology in past and present societies serves as perhaps the best way to keep the disagreement alive—preventing the risk of losing this complexity to official narratives. As anthropologist Flores delineates, "Memory-place, and its physical and concrete evidence, validates and authenticates a specter of the past, whereas official history—intent on unraveling the temporal movement of the past with its sources and archives—is only as solid as the narrative it produces." Ironically, in attempting to cleanse the contested history of the United States and the world, those opposed to the Manhattan Project National Historic Park could allow for the flourishing of a simplified official narrative as outlined by Flores, thus running the risk of what Lowenthal alerts: "Credence in a mythic past crafted for some present cause flies in the face of the past's actual complexity and precludes impartial historical knowledge."

Since the moment of the bomb's creation, vigorous debate has ensued about whether or not its use was necessary, justified, and ethical; opposition to dropping the atomic bomb came from all sides of the political spectrum, including Protestant and Catholic spokespeople, *National Review*, *Time*, *New York Times*, and *U.S. News* and—perhaps most remarkably—some scientists involved in the Manhattan Project. Without the well-established emotional impact of standing and learning at the historic site itself, these historic and contemporary disputes could be lost to seemingly inevitable and obvious narratives constructed by straightforward official histories, the nature and worrisome effect of which John Michael Vlach articulately outlines and captures in the context of American slavery:

> *The difficulty and awkwardness that most Americans experience when discussing the history of racial slavery in the United States can be traced... to the inadequate textbooks that they are compelled to read while in high school... The authors of these volumes generally recount the dramatic events of America's formation in such bland diction that these books become the printed equivalents of "mumbling lectures." Further, by being so committed to positive and uplifting portrayals, these writers unwaveringly follow a "progress as usual" story line and thus treat our long history of slavery as merely a temporary aberration that had no lasting consequences. Such an approach not only marginalizes slavery and its attendant racist ideology but also marks the topic as one requiring no further discussion.*

Applied to nuclear history, this type of manifest and predestined narrative would not only obscure the contested history of nuclear weapons but also, as a result, reduce the viability and vitality of a continued discussion about the validity of nuclear technology.[61]

---

[61] Richard Flores, *Remembering the Alamo: Memory,*

The professional study of history no longer reveres but instead remembers its subjects of study; professional historic preservation reflects the same sober analysis, especially in the National Park Service. Max Page and Randall Mason, who work in many disciplines including history, note, "The academic field of American history has been fundamentally transformed over the past generation. Historians now routinely seek out the variety of perspectives on a particular time or place, and we value many formerly invisible and disturbing aspects of our history." The National Park Service reflects this growth in appreciation of more diverse perspectives to develop more complicated narratives. Linenthal affirms, "At Gettysburg, diverse ceremonies at the 125th anniversary in 1988 revealed different readings of the meaning of the Civil War. Growing sensitivity to less-heroic interpretations of

---

Modernity, and the Master Symbol (Austin: University of Texas Press, 2002), 21; David Lowenthal, "The Heritage Crusade and Its Contradictions," in Max Page and Randall Mason, eds., *Giving Preservation a History: Histories of Historic Preservation in the United States* (New York: Routledge, 2004), 21; Edward T. Linenthal, "Anatomy of a Controversy," in Edward T. Linenthal and Tom Engelhardt, eds., *History Wars: The Enola Gay and Other Battles for the American Past* (New York: Henry Holt and Company, 1996), 10-11; John Michael Vlach, "The Last Great Taboo Subject: Exhibiting Slavery at the Library of Congress," James Oliver Horton and Lois E. Horton, eds., *Slavery and Public History: The Tough Stuff of American Memory* (New York: The New Press, 2006), 57.

the Anglo-American frontier has profoundly altered the National Park Service's interpretation of the significance of the Battle of the Little Bighorn. And at Pearl Harbor, the Park Service is charged with interpreting a site that for many is still an 'open wound.'" Clearly, the National Park Service has demonstrated its ability to change over time and to adapt to fresh and multifaceted interpretations. It remains the American institution at "the forefront of historic preservation," as historian Hal Rothman acknowledges, and it has matured over several decades: "After being keepers of the ceremonial landscapes during the 1920s, the Park Service had become guardians of a cultural heritage." Indeed, the National Park Service has proven itself the appropriate custodian of the vital historic sites and stories related to the Manhattan Project. Janice Dubel, a human rights activist throughout Asia, recognizes the tackling of critical interpretations by the National Park Service at Manzanar National Historic Site, which "represents Japanese-Americans who were presumed guilty wholly on the basis of their race." The NPS would employ the same judiciousness in interpreting nuclear history at the Manhattan Project National Historical Park.[62]

---

[62] Max Page and Randall Mason, "Rethinking the Roots of the Historic Preservation Movement," in Max Page and Randall Mason, eds., *Giving Preservation a History: Histories of Historic Preservation in the United States* (New York: Routledge, 2004), 15; Edward Tabor Linenthal, *Sacred Ground: Americans and Their*

Professional historical interpretation understands its role of presenting complicated narratives that connect the audience to the historic resource and thus spark awareness, research, contemplation, and discussion. The iconic philosopher of interpretation, Freeman Tilden, proclaimed over half a century ago, "The chief aim of interpretation is not instruction, but provocation... The purpose of interpretation is to stimulate the reader or hearer toward a desire to widen his horizon of interests and knowledge, and to gain an

---

Battlefields (Champaign: University of Illinois Press, 1991, 1993), 6; Hal Rothman, *America's National Monuments: The Politics of Preservation* (Lawrence: University Press of Kansas, 1989), 209, 188; Janice L. Dubel, "Remembering a Japanese-American Concentration Camp at Manzanar National Historic Site," in Paul A. Shackel, ed., *Myth, Memory, and the Making of the American Landscape* (Gainesville: University Press of Florida, 2001), 100. Edward T. Linenthal, who was involved as a historian with Little Bighorn Battlefield National Monument in the 1980s, also refers to the effort to "transform the Little Bighorn battlefield from a shrine to George A. Custer and the Seventh Cavalry into a historic site where different – often clashing – stories could be told... I had watched as a complex interpretation of a mythic American event had successfully supplanted an enduring 'first take,'" in Edward T. Linenthal, "Anatomy of a Controversy," in Edward T. Linenthal and Tom Engelhardt, eds., *History Wars: The Enola Gay and Other Battles for the American Past* (New York: Henry Holt and Company, 1996), 9.

understanding of the greater truths that lie behind any statements of fact." Tilden's six principles of interpretation still serve as the basis for interpretive planning in the National Park Service. He realized, "A cardinal purpose of interpretation… is to present a whole rather than a part, no matter how interesting the specific part may be." Larger whole stories of which the Manhattan Project is an integral part surround the themes of scientific achievement, energy production, military history, government secrecy, executive power, international relations, Cold War, and global reconfiguration.[63]

A respected federal institution had already been blocked from interpreting these pervasive historical themes nearly two decades prior to the failed congressional vote on the Manhattan Project National Historical Park Act. The 1995 *Enola Gay* exhibit in the Smithsonian National Air and Space Museum demonstrated the perils of confronting the interpretation of these contested historical themes, and the reaction that it sparked only further reinforced the timeliness and relevance of ensuring continued preservation and interpretation of this historical moment. Richard Kohn, the renowned military historian who helped advise the exhibit's plan, considers the cancellation of this exhibit "one of the worst tragedies to befall the public presentation of

---

[63] Freeman Tilden, *Interpreting Our Heritage* (Chapel Hill: University of North Carolina Press, 1957, 1967, 1977, 2007), 35, 59, 35, 68.

history in the United States in this generation... [It] forfeited an opportunity to educate a worldwide audience of millions about one of the century's defining experiences." As with the risk inflicted upon the National Park Service by the failure of the House of Representatives to establish the Manhattan Project National Historical Park, the Smithsonian's integrity was compromised: "Thus one of the premier cultural institutions of the United States and its foremost museum system surrendered its scholarly independence and a significant amount of its authority in American intellectual life to accommodate to a political perspective." These implications are far-reaching, as Kohn surmises, "If the idea that everything is politics now colors American cultural life, civic discourse could begin to succumb to the suppression characteristic of the totalitarian regimes Americans have fought and died to defeat." Still more worrisome, Kohn warns, "Unable to explore their past openly or critically, Americans might endanger their political system and damage the liberty on which that system is based and which it is designed to preserve."[64]

Despite the retirement from the Senate of the park bill's greatest champion and co-sponsor, Jeff

---

[64] Richard H. Kohn, "History at Risk: The Case of the *Enola Gay*," in Edward T. Linenthal and Tom Engelhardt, eds., *History Wars: The Enola Gay and Other Battles for the American Past* (New York: Henry Holt and Company, 1996), 140, 141.

Bingaman, the 113th Congress retained some key supporting voices, and the bill ultimately passed. There is consensus by all parties regarding the significance of the Manhattan Project, as the intense disputes surrounding its commemoration remind us—and that's where the sides can agree to use as a core from which to build. Applying the latest theories and practices of historic preservation are necessary; the field of historic preservation has grown to grapple with varied and complicated perspectives. The National Park Service is the fitting entity to execute this challenging, momentous, and expert task. It has proven its capability and willingness to offer diverse viewpoints about multifaceted stories that carry emotional charge. Omitting perhaps the most transformative event of the twentieth-century from the national narrative due to a sense of shame reveals an immature lack of responsibility and deliberate manipulation and distortion of its record on the part of the nation-state in order to avoid confronting its past. Such a glaring exclusion also compromises the integrity and respectability of the National Park Service. Opportunities are vast for thoughtful interpretation and education to spark worthwhile and relevant reflection and conversation. The Manhattan Project National Historical Park creates a forum unlike anything else could.

Afterword

Wrestling with History

Grappling with our past – particularly when it is unsavory or controversial – can be fraught with risk. We Americans have a certain image of ourselves, as protectors of freedom, liberators; champions of the idea that all people are created equal. Therefore, it can be jarring and upsetting when we are confronted with our complicity in African American slavery, Jim Crow, the Indian removal of the 1830s, treatment of Chinese immigrants in the late 19th Century, the internment of Japanese-Americans in World War 2, and other unsettling stories. No nation is without complications, or dark periods, in its history. How we deal with these complex and controversial stories is crucial to the health of a nation. When we bury our past beneath triumphant, blemish-free narratives, we conceal the truth and hold back the nation. Only when we lay bare our history, and wrestle with its unpleasant moments do we begin to understand who we are, how we came to our beliefs, and how we can move forward. When President Abraham Lincoln said in the first sentence of his Gettysburg Address, "Four score and seven years ago, our fathers brought forth on this continent a new nation, conceived in liberty and dedicated to the proposition that all men were created equal," not only did nearly half of the country fiercely disagree with this statement, they were fighting a war in opposition to the idea of equality. Lincoln was speaking not of who we were, but of who we could be and who we should be.

Toward the end of this fine book, Raffi Andonian quotes Freeman Tilden, the father of interpretation in the National Park Service, who famously wrote that interpretation "is not instruction but provocation." This is what Lincoln did so superbly in his Gettysburg Address; he challenged people to think about what our nation believed in. This is what National Park historical sites can do well; they can create a meaningful dialogue and understanding that avoids the slogans and shouting and celebration we are often prone to in society today. It was not always this way in the NPS. When I started with the agency in the summer of 1979 at Gettysburg National Military Park (NMP), the park's theme was "The High Water Mark," essentially a narrative that focused not on the important consequences of Union victory in the battle and the war, but instead on the Confederacy and how its defeat had been that short nation's turning point. The emphasis was on the courage of the fighting men on both sides and the crucial decisions that caused Robert E. Lee and the Confederates to lose the battle. It was a safe narrative in which everyone fought the good fight for what they believed in. Missing from this narrative was any mention about what Union victory meant; an end to slavery in America and preservation of the Union. It was possible for a visitor to tour the park's visitor center and Cyclorama

Center, which contained a massive panorama of Pickett's Charge by a French artist completed in 1882, take a two-hour tour of the battlefield and attend a ranger led program, and never once learn what the war was about and what was at stake. We softened the cause of the war and its most controversial subject – African American slavery – by focusing on safe topics. If visitors encountered anything about what the two armies were fighting about – Union and slavery – they could select from a smorgasbord of reasons, all presented as equal in significance. A visitor might choose to believe it was slavery, or state's rights, or tariffs, or just differences between the two sections of the country. This might have comforted those who wished to sideline or dismiss slavery as a cause of the war, but it was poor history and not sustained by scholarship. The tariff was irrelevant in 1860 and state's rights was simply a defense of slavery. The slave states supported a strong central government when it benefitted them. As for the differences between the two sections of the country, slavery was the central distinction.

In the early 1990s the National Park Service began to address its failure to interpret complicated stories at its historic sites by broadening its interpretive stories based on scholarship rather than on what made people comfortable. At Gettysburg we began to discuss slavery's centrality to the war. At Little Big Horn, the park changed its name from Custer National Monument to Little Big Horn National Monument, and began to interpret the stories of both Native Americans and the army sent to enforce the policies of the U.S. government. This era also began to see new historic sites added to the National Park system that interpreted controversial subjects; Little Rock Central High School National Historic Site, Manzanar National Historic Site, Martin Luther King NHP, Harriet Tubman Underground Railroad NHP, and many others. These changes occurred gradually and were not always greeted warmly. I recall a phone call I received from a woman in South Carolina who declared to me that she was boycotting Gettysburg because we were now teaching "politically correct" history and would not be talking about the battle anymore. I replied that I was sorry she would not visit the park again and pointed out that we were still interpreting the battle primarily but wanted visitors to understand what the war was about. I also pointed out that she had it backward; we had been doing "politically correct" history that made one group of people feel comfortable for years. Now, we were confronting the story that overwhelming scholarship tells us caused the war, and trying to understand it without casting blame on individuals.

Interpreting controversial and complicated subjects for the general public can be tricky. When we were planning the new museum that opened at Gettysburg NMP in 2008, we spent a great deal of time thinking about how to present the story of why the war came, what it was about, and its consequences. We included in our planning a scholars advisory board of some of the country's top Civil War academics and curators, including Gary

Gallagher, Eric Foner, James McPherson and Nina Silber. In the end we decided to let the participants speak for themselves. Visitors would encounter many points of view from the letters, speeches, newspapers, congressional debates, diaries and journals of common people and principal leaders. We did not need to tell people that slavery led to secession and war – the people on both sides who lived through it said it loud and clear. It is harder to argue against original sources. This does not mean the Gettysburg museum was without controversy. We received numerous verbal complaints and complaint cards, almost exclusively from individuals who were furious that the NPS dared to tell such a lie that slavery was the cause of secession and war. Some were also disturbed by the closing film with its thought-provoking and somewhat troubling story of the war's consequences. One of the complaint cards we received included an email address. I sent the person all the secession declarations that seceding states published and asked her if after reading them she still believed slavery had nothing to do with the war. She responded, somewhat grudgingly, that maybe it did, but this individual still wanted to mistrust the government. But at least her experience in the museum caused provocation and made her think.

When Raffi Andonian worked with me at Gettysburg NMP he created an extremely challenging interactive talk which he presented at our evening campfire program, about the Confederate battle flag. This was the flag carried into battle by combat units of the Army of Northern Virginia and is the flag embraced by racists in this country in the 20th and 21st centuries. To say the subject is controversial is an understatement, yet Raffi demonstrated it was possible to have an informative, constructive discussion about a subject fraught with emotion. He did this by being well informed about the history of the flag and trying to understand its history rather than seeking to condemn or defend it. He did not provide absolute answers, instead he encouraged dialogue and thinking. This is the fine line National Park Service interpreters and exhibits must walk, but they do it well all across the service. This is also what Raffi Andonian does with this book. He challenges us to think.

Congressman's Dennis Kucinich's statement, quoted in this book, that the creation of Manhattan National Historic Park would only "celebrate ingenuity that was used to put all humanity at risk," is precisely the opposite of what national parks today do when they interpret history. We do not "celebrate" Gettysburg or Antietam or Little Big Horn. These were terrible tragedies. We seek to understand them and what they mean and how they shaped our country and our lives.

This is what national parks can do. It is what Raffi has done with this book.

D. Scott Hartwig,
Gettysburg, Pennsylvania

Bibliography

Gar Alperovitz, *Atomic Diplomacy: Hiroshima and Potsdam: The Use of the Atomic Bomb and the American Confrontation with Soviet Power* (New York: Simon & Schuster, 1965).

Gar Alperovitz, *The Decision to Use the Atomic Bomb and the Architecture of an American Myth* (New York: Alfred A. Knopf, 1995).

"Art after Fukushima," *The Economist*, 10 March 2012.

"Atomic Bomb Labs May Be Made a National Park," *CBS This Morning*, aired 6 August 2012, and available at http://www.cbsnews.com/video/watch/?id=741729 2n .

David Barna, "Mainichi Daily News (Tokyo): Hiroshima, Nagasaki Express Concern about Manhattan Project Plan," http://webmail.itc.nps.gov/pipermail/infozone/201 1-December/001727.html .

Barbara Bender, "Introduction," in Barbara Bender and Margot Winer, eds., *Contested Landscapes: Movement, Exile and Place* (Oxford: Berg, 2001).

Robert Bevan, *The Destruction of Memory: Architecture at War* (London: Reaktion Books, 2006).

Kai Bird and Lawrence Lifschultz, eds., *Hiroshima's Shadow* (Stony Creek: Pamphleteer's Press, 1998).

William J. Broad, "Bid to Preserve Manhattan Project Sites in a Park Stirs Debate," *The New York Times*, 3 December 2012.

Mary C. Byers, "In the Beginning," *History of the Los Alamos Historical Society and Museum, 1968-1988* (Los Alamos: Los Alamos Historical Society, May 1988).

Jackie Cabasso, "UFPJ Applauds Dennis Kucinich for Leading Defeat of Bill in U.S. House of Representatives to Establish Manhattan Project National Park," United for Peace and Justice, 16 October 2012, http://www.unitedforpeace.org/2012/10/16/ufpj-applauds-dennis-kucinich-for-leading-defeat-of-bill-in-u-s-house-of-representatives-to-establish-manhattan-project-national-park .

Amy Cole, "The Manhattan Project: 20th Century History, 21st Century Significance," *PreservationNation Blog*, National Trust for Historic Preservation, 19 July 2012, http://blog.preservationnation.org/2012/07/19/the-manhattan-project-20th-century-history-21st-century-significance/#.UP5dzq6Oivg .

Greg Dickinson, Carole Blair, and Brian L. Ott, "Rhetoric/Memory/Place," in Greg Dickinson, Carole Blair, and Brian L. Ott, eds., *Places of Public Memory: The Rhetoric of Museums and Memorials* (Tuscaloosa: University of Alabama Press, 2010).

Jim DiPeso, "Pass the Bill Establishing Manhattan Project
National Historical Park," *The Huffington Post*, 26
September 2012,
http://www.huffingtonpost.com/jim-
dipeso/manhattan-project-national-historical-
park_b_1917059.html .

John Dower, *War Without Mercy: Race and Power in the
Pacific War* (New York: Pantheon, 1986).

Janice L. Dubel, "Remembering a Japanese-American
Concentration Camp at Manzanar National
Historic Site," in Paul A. Shackel, ed., *Myth,
Memory, and the Making of the American
Landscape* (Gainesville: University Press of
Florida, 2001).

Editorial Board, "Commemorating the Bomb," *The
Washington Post*, 12 August 2012.

Editorial Board, "Manhattan Project National Park Would
Commemorate History, Not Glorify It," *The
Boston Globe*, 7 December 2012.

Tom Engelhardt and Edward T. Linenthal, "Introduction:
History Under Siege," in Edward T. Linenthal and
Tom Engelhardt, eds., *History Wars: The Enola
Gay and Other Battles for the American Past*
(New York: Henry Holt and Company, 1996).

Herbert Feis, *The Atomic Bomb and the End of World War
II* (Princeton: Princeton University Press, 1961,
1966).

James Marston Fitch, *Historic Preservation: Curatorial Management of the Built World* (New York: McGraw-Hill, 1982).

Richard Flores, *Remembering the Alamo: Memory, Modernity, and the Master Symbol* (Austin: University of Texas Press, 2002).

Alonzo L. Hamby, *Man of the People: A Life of Harry S. Truman* (New York: Oxford University Press, 1995).

"Hiroshima, Nagasaki Concerned Manhattan," *House of Japan*, 3 December 2011, http://www.houseofjapan.com/local/hiroshima-nagasaki-concerned-manhattan .

How to Apply the National Register Criteria for Evaluation, National Register Bulletin 15, National Park Service, Department of the Interior, accessed on 1 March 2013 via http://www.nps.gov/history/nr/publications/bulletins/nrb15/ .

Ashutosh Jogalekar, "On the Uselessness of Nuclear Weapons," *Scientific American*, 13 January 2013.

Richard H. Kohn, "History at Risk: The Case of the *Enola Gay*," in Edward T. Linenthal and Tom Engelhardt, eds., *History Wars: The Enola Gay and Other Battles for the American Past* (New York: Henry Holt and Company, 1996).

Andrew Lass, "Romantic Documents and Political
    Monuments: The Meaning-Fulfillment
    of History in 19th-Century Czech Nationalism,"
    American Ethnologist 15 (3), 1988, p. 467.

Edward T. Linenthal, "Anatomy of a Controversy," in
    Edward T. Linenthal and Tom Engelhardt, eds.,
    *History Wars: The Enola Gay and Other Battles
    for the American Past* (New York: Henry Holt and
    Company, 1996).

Edward Tabor Linenthal, *Sacred Ground: Americans and
    Their Battlefields* (Champaign: University of
    Illinois Press, 1991, 1993).

Los Alamos Historical Society, *History of the Los Alamos
    Ranch School*, accessed via
    http://www.losalamoshistory.org/school.htm
    on 4 January 2013.

Los Alamos Historical Society, Los Alamos County, and
    Fuller Lodge/Historic Districts Advisory Board,
    Los Alamos Homestead Tour, brochure, 2012.

Los Alamos Scientific Laboratory, *Los Alamos: Beginning
    of an Era, 1943-1945* (Los Alamos: Los Alamos
    Historical Society, 2008).

David Lowenthal, "The Heritage Crusade and Its
    Contradictions," in Max Page and Randall Mason,
    eds., *Giving Preservation a History: Histories of
    Historic Preservation in the United States* (New
    York: Routledge, 2004).

David Lowenthal, *The Past Is a Foreign Country*
    (Cambridge: Cambridge University Press, 1985).

Robert James Maddox, *Weapons for Victory: The Hiroshima Decision Fifty Years Later* (Columbia: University of Missouri Press, 1995).

David McCullough, *Truman* (New York: Simon & Schuster, 1992).

Dale McFeatters, "McFeatters: Turn Manhattan Project Sites into National Parks," N*ewsday*, 3 August 2012.

Jennifer McStotts, "Preserving Walls: Cultural Landscapes with Divisive Histories," Cari Goetcheus and Eric MacDonald, eds., *Exploring the Boundaries of Historic Landscape Preservation*, Proceedings of the Twenty-ninth Annual Meeting of the Alliance for Historic Landscape Preservation 2007 (Clemson: Clemson University Digital Press, 2008).

Denise D. Meringolo, *Museums, Monuments, and National Parks: Toward a New Genealogy of Public History* (Amherst: University of Massachusetts Press, 2012).

Randi Minetor, "Manhattan Project Park Bill Achieves Majority, but Fails in the House," *Examiner*, 21 September 2012.

William J. Murtagh, *Keeping Time: The History and Theory of Preservation in America* (New York: Sterling Publishing Co., 1988).

National Historic Landmarks Survey, National Park
Service, accessed on 1 March 2013 via
http://www.nps.gov/nhl/designations/Lists/NM01.
pdf .

Robert S. Nelson and Margaret Olin, "Introduction," in
Robert S. Nelson and Margaret Olin, eds.,
Monuments and Memory, Made and Unmade
(Chicago: University of Chicago Press, 2013).

Robert P. Newman, *Enola Gay and the Court of History*
(New York: Peter Lang Publishing, 2004).

Robert P. Newman, *Truman and the Hiroshima Cult* (East
Lansing: Michigan State University Press, 1995).

"Nuclear Power: The 30-Year Itch," *The Economist*, 18
February 2012.

Max Page and Randall Mason, "Rethinking the Roots of
the Historic Preservation Movement," in Max
Page and Randall Mason, eds., *Giving
Preservation a History: Histories of Historic
Preservation in the United States* (New York:
Routledge, 2004).

Richard Rhodes, *The Making of the Atomic Bomb* (New
York: Simon & Schuster, 1986).

Alois Riegl, "The Modern Cult of Monuments: Its
Character and Its Origin," translated by Forster
and Ghirardo, *Oppositions* 25 (Fall 1982).

Ted Robbins, "Manhattan Project Sites Part of Proposed Park," National Public Radio, 4 December 2012, transcript, http://www.npr.org/templates/transcript/transcript.php?storyId=166402093 .

"Roos Says A-Bomb Park Reflective, Not Celebratory," *The Japan Times*, 25 January 2012.

Hal Rothman, *America's National Monuments: The Politics of Preservation* (Lawrence: University Press of Kansas, 1989).

Alfred Runte, *National Parks: The American Experience* (Lincoln: University of Nebraska Press, 1979, 1987).

Julian Ryall, "US Forced to Defend Manhattan Project Park to Japan," *The Telegraph*, 25 January 2012.

Dave Simon, "Manhattan Project National Park Is Controversial, but Necessary," *The Santa Fe New Mexican*, 30 July 2011.

Richard Simon, "A-Bomb Park Bill Fails in House," *Albuquerque Journal*, 22 September 2012.

Richard Simon, "House Effort to Recognize the A-Bomb Is a Dud," *Los Angeles Times*, 20 September 2012.

Richard Simon, "House Rejects Manhattan Project Park Bill," *Journal North*, 21 September 2012.

Richard Simon, "U.S. House Effort to Recognize the Atomic Bomb with New National Park Is a Dud," *The Dallas Morning News*, 20 September 2012.

D. Ray Smith, "Historically Speaking: Putting the Manhattan Project into Proper Perspective," *The Oak Ridger*, 8 October 2012.

Ronald Takaki, *Hiroshima: Why America Dropped the Atomic Bomb* (Boston: Little, Brown & Company, 1995).

"The Dream that Failed," Special Report on Nuclear Energy, *The Economist*, 10 March 2012.

The New Mexican, "Manhattan Project Park Should Be Shelved," *The Santa Fe New Mexican*, 24 July 2011.

Freeman Tilden, *Interpreting Our Heritage* (Chapel Hill: University of North Carolina Press, 1957, 1967, 1977, 2007).

J. E. Tunbridge and G. J. Ashworth, *Dissonant Heritage: The Management of the Past as a Resource in Conflict* (Chichester: John Wiley & Sons, 1996).

"U.S. Ambassador to Japan Defends MP National Historical Park," Atomic Heritage Foundation, 25 January 2012, http://www.atomicheritage.org/index.php/ahf-updates-mainmenu-153/628-us-ambassador-to-japan-defends-manhattan-project-national-historical-park.html .

"US Tells Hiroshima Manhattan Project Park Plan Not Celebratory," *House of Japan*, 25 January 2012, Http://www.houseofjapan.com/local/us-tells-hiroshima-manhattan-project-park-plan-not-celebratory .

John Michael Vlach, "The Last Great Taboo Subject: Exhibiting Slavery at the Library of Congress," James Oliver Horton and Lois E. Horton, eds., *Slavery and Public History: The Tough Stuff of American Memory* (New York: The New Press, 2006).

Dennis D. Wainstock, *The Decision to Drop the Atomic Bomb* (Westport: Praeger Publishers, 1996).

J. Samuel Walker, "Recent Literature on Truman's Atomic Bomb Decision: A Search for Middle Ground," *Diplomatic History*, Vol. 29, No. 2, April 2005, pp. 311-334.

Lore Watt, "The Society Continues," *History of the Los Alamos Historical Society and Museum, 1968-1988* (Los Alamos: Los Alamos Historical Society, May 1988).

Ward Wilson, *Five Myths About Nuclear Weapons* (New York: Houghton Mifflin Harcourt, 2013).